UNISON – the Envy of its Competitors

UNIS🌐N -the Envy of its Competitors

The Origins, Rise and Eventual Decline
of the UNISON Network

IAN MACALPINE-LENY

With Drawings by Javier Barcaiztegui (BARCA)

HAGGERSTON PRESS

Copies may be ordered from

Ian Macalpine-Leny, The Old Rectory,
Doddington, LN6 4RU (UK)

or

Rudi Portaria, 4612 Muirwood Place,
Stow OH 44224 (USA)

Price, including p & p, £20 or €30 or $30.

ISBN 1 869812 21 2

Printed in Great Britain at St Edmundsbury Press,
Bury St Edmunds

Contents

Illustrations

IT TAKES **TWO** TO TANGO!

BARCA.
June 91. Madrid.

*Santi Gil de Biedma & Joe Roxe on completion of the acquisition
of 50 per cent of Gil y Carvajal by J&H*

Preface

Ian Macalpine-Leny has asked me to write a few lines as a preface to his book about UNISON. I am really grateful to him, and for all of us who lived through the times he describes, the book will be tremendously exciting.

There is no doubt that being part of UNISON was a remarkable experience. Some of the most important insurance brokers of the Western World decided to set up a unique alliance, with no kind of contractual link and almost no cross-ownership, and anybody reading the book will be fascinated by this feat.

I suspect that I was the only chief executive who represented his company (Gil y Carvajal) at all the annual meetings of UNISON – called, tongue-in-cheek, Heads of State Summits! I was twenty-eight when I first became involved in UNISON and finished when I was in my sixties: a whole working life though, writing these lines, I am still active as Chairman of Aon Gil y Carvajal.

Like Ian, I could also tell plenty of stories. But after all, looking backwards, what has been really important has been the true partnership between our firms, with never a dispute, the real brotherhood developed amongst our people at all levels, and the very highest technical and professional standards set, still remembered with admiration in the insurance world.

UNISON was a great adventure, in which we had a lot of fun, made lasting friendships, and of course worked hard for our clients, for whom we provided an unrivalled service. For any young professional who reads this book, there is a clear message which – in my opinion – will always remain valuable and relevant.

UNISON has been a most important part of my life, and just writing these words brings me deep emotion.

Santiago Gil de Biedma
Madrid, May 2004

9

Ian Macalpine-Leny

Author's Note

I'm glad you've decided to read this bit too because it enables me to get a number of things off my chest.

It has fallen on me to be the somewhat unlikely chronicler of the most successful international servicing network the insurance industry has yet seen, since I was lucky enough to be on the stage for the Golden Years between 1980 and 1990. As I have always found reading about insurance immensely boring, I have avoided describing in detail how UNISON acquired and serviced business around the world. Instead I have written about what interested me: the people, and some of their more amusing exploits.

It is very difficult to write a book like this without offending someone. Most of us are not used to reading about ourselves in print, and if you are not described in the way you see yourself, I can only apologise. Likewise, some of the events may not appear as you recollect them. All I can say is that I have gone to a lot of trouble to establish versions of events from those who were actually there, and time plays tricks on the memories of us all. I do make a number of observations both directly and indirectly. These are mine and mine alone. I would be delighted to discuss them with you, if you are prepared to buy me lunch.

I have quoted extensively from Dorrance Sexton's account, written after he retired, of the beginnings of Johnson & Higgins' international operations. Sadly he is no longer around to ask, but as the instigator of what became the European network and eventually UNISON, I would like to think that he would have been only too pleased to be quoted. I did get permission from Emil Kratovil, in his intensive-care bed in a Greenwich hospital just before he died, to reproduce his brilliant *Ballad of Water and Wall*.

This book would not have been possible without the help of a huge number of people who have given me taped interviews, sent stories or anecdotes, or helped and encouraged me in some way. I am deeply grateful to them all, and they are acknowledged in Appendix I. In addition, nothing would have got beyond my computer screen if it hadn't been for the generosity of the subscribers who put down a line on the Slip to pay for the publication of this book.

I owe a huge debt of gratitude to Ken Seward, my long-suffering editor, to Peter Ledger, Michael Claydon and Nick Davenport who read my draft and made many helpful suggestions and corrections, and to Rudi Portaria who painstakingly assembled the biographies in Appendix I. I am also indebted to Bob Hatcher, David Palmer, Michael Day and Chip Bechtold who kindly lent originals of some of the illustrations. Lastly and most importantly, I must thank my good friend Javier Barcaiztegui who had the original idea, and whose brilliant drawings, all of which were originally drawn during UNISON meetings, bring the whole thing to life. Well known in Spain as the caricaturist "BARCA", Javier was a leading member of UNISON from the time he became responsible for Gil y Carvajal international in 1979, until it all ended in 1997.

Ian Macalpine-Leny
Doddington, May 2004

1 Prologue

This is the story of a global insurance broker network, but that is largely incidental. The problems faced, the solutions found, and the lessons learned are equally applicable to any global network. This is what makes the whole UNISON story so fascinating, and worthy of a wider audience.

What made this network stand apart was that against the perceived wisdom of the day, it was based not on common ownership but on a common commitment to excellence, the members joining because they wanted to, not because they were forced. Perhaps more importantly, they all believed in putting the customer, any customer of the network, first. This resulted for the clients in the finest and most professional servicing network that the financial services industry has yet seen. What the competition simply couldn't understand was how this network could stay together, let alone be way ahead of its time in innovation, service, and control.

The answer lies in these pages. The magic ingredient, the glue that held the whole thing together, was the people. This book tells the story of how far-sighted and inspired partners of an American brokerage firm progressively put together a network across the globe that became, quite simply, the envy of its competitors. And of the fun we all had doing it.

2 The Reason Why

Let us begin, in the words of the King of Hearts in *Alice in Wonderland*, at the beginning. There have been brokers ever since business began, but it was in the world of insurance that the task of bringing together a buyer and a seller, in this case a client and an insurance underwriter, saw broking develop into a highly specialised business of its own. This came to attract, particularly in the UK, some of the most brilliant and colourful characters of their time. For many years it was highly profitable, depended very much on personal contacts, and tended to appeal to intelligent extroverts who often didn't have any particular specialist skills, or sometimes very little else for that matter. Just as well, because basic insurance broking was never rocket science. As one Lloyd's broker remarked, broking is rather like sex – you can either do it, or you can't; you don't have to be taught.

In the beginnings of the marine insurance business in the 17th century in London, brokers as such were unknown. The ship owners wanted to know exactly who was underwriting the risks on their ships, and placed the business themselves. But as values grew larger, and the settlement of marine insurance claims became more complex, specialists developed who made their living from adjusting marine claims. These so-called average adjusters started to branch out into placing business on behalf of their clients, and so gave rise to the first insurance brokers, who dealt only with marine business.

The leading marine brokerage firm in the USA was Johnson and Higgins, universally known as J&H, headquartered in New York. J&H had been fabulously profitable, and in the 1920s and 1930s one of the directors was among the wealthiest men in the USA. But almost exclusive focus on marine business and the static structure of the board, some of whom were in their seventies, took its toll, especially when the US marine fleets were dramatically reduced in size at the end of World War II.* All of a sudden the directors realised that they were being overtaken

* 'J&H International Operations 1952–1972', p7.

14

by upstart brokers such as Marsh & McLennan who had started to concentrate on business other than marine.

J&H came out of the doldrums when Elmer Jefferson became president in 1952.* He had started in the mailroom at fourteen, and went on to become chairman and CEO. Under his leadership, J&H commenced a period of considerable growth. But although Jefferson's leadership made it possible, it was the vision of Dorrance Sexton that set the company on the path of international business. Sexton had joined in 1933, the son of a serving J&H director. This raised eyebrows considerably at the time, because there was a strict no nepotism rule to prevent preferential hiring. But Sexton won the respect of all his colleagues by ability and sheer hard work, and was elected to the board in 1949.

When Jefferson took the reins, J&H had operations in two other countries, Cuba and Canada. The office in Havana had been opened in 1922 and, although small, was extremely profitable, looking after many of the sugar mills on the island as well as major local industrial companies. All this was to change under Castro. The manager Charlie Charlesworth and his assistant Paul Pinkham returned to New York in 1960 when the business was nationalised. The Canadian office, which had been opened in Montreal in 1906,† was always rather an enigma, because it was treated by the J&H board as an extension of the US and responsibility remained with New York. Marine placements in the Lloyd's and London markets were made by Willis Faber in London, and the small number of overseas fleets that had used J&H for placements in the US market had disappeared after the war.

Dorrance Sexton, who succeeded Jefferson in 1962, was straight out of central casting. Tall, good-looking, urbane and witty, he was the sort of man you immediately noticed when he came into the room. He was persuaded by a good friend who had spent a year in Brazil that although the country was fifty years behind the US economically, it was about to take off, and so was the perfect place for J&H to open an office. Further, he

* ibid.
† Originally in Willis's office, moving to separate premises in 1909.

15

knew just the man to do this: Harry Wentworth Hollmeyer. This was greeted with great scepticism by the J&H board, the majority of whom were still marine directors. It has to be remembered that J&H had only opened two new offices since the 1920s, Toronto and Pittsburgh, and closed three more in the 1930s, Boston, Baltimore and New Orleans; in spite of the operations in Canada and Cuba, they had effectively no experience of truly international operations; and, last but not least, the twenty-two hours from New York to Rio de Janeiro via Venezuela by DC6 was not exactly a commuter flight.* Quite apart from this, there was a certain amount of doubt as to how a country that effectively had no brokers would respond to the aggressive US way of doing business. But Elmer Jefferson gave the project his whole-hearted support, and was able to convince the board. There was then a delay of a couple of years while Hollmeyer recovered from an attack of polio, so it was not until 1954 that J&H opened up in Rio as a joint venture with Deltec, a South American financial organisation based in Brazil. This partnership formed the pattern for the subsequent expansion of J&H into Latin America.

Sexton couldn't have appointed a better man than Hollmeyer. A Marine Corps fighter pilot in World War II, he proved to be an extremely able leader and administrator, and during the twenty-nine years that he led J&H Brazil it rose to be the third largest operation after New York and Los Angeles. That now famous remark of Elmer Jefferson back in 1954 – 'It's a different basket, and maybe one day we'll find some eggs in it' – couldn't have been more true.

Buoyed by the success of the Brazilian operation, Sexton then turned to Venezuela. In 1956 J&H bought the business of Harry Mason, who had established a brokerage operation in the booming capital, Caracas. A young marine cargo man was sent down from New York to help Mason with the integration process. Six months later, Mason suffered a debilitating stroke, and Bill Bumsted took over the management. In addition to Bumsted, J&H in Venezuela also boasted Jack Groene (whose company in Puerto la Cruz J&H bought), Ken Withers, Ken

* 'J&H International Operations 1952–1972', p8.

16

Seward and Hugh Hausman, whom we'll hear all about later.

With Brazil and Venezuela running satisfactorily, Sexton now turned his attention to the third-largest industrialised country in South America, Argentina. About that time, purely by chance, Walter Smink, Ernie Gould and Gordon Grundy decided to leave the O'Grady Lloyd's Agency to set up on their own. Harry Hollmeyer persuaded them to join J&H and start J&H Argentina instead. Premises were provided by Deltec and business commenced in 1960. Ernie Gould was subsequently asked to go and set up J&H Chile, where despite the serious economic problems in that country he proved to be an extremely effective manager.

Deltec had meanwhile opened in Peru, and asked J&H to join them. Sexton did not consider there was sufficient potential and declined, so Deltec started their own brokerage firm, Consultores de Seguros. Inevitably J&H got drawn in to the management, but negotiations to buy the company were never concluded. That leaves Colombia. In the 1950s Gordon Lawry, a young American who had been with American International Underwriters (AIU), set up his own broking operation in Bogotá. As J&H needed representation in Colombia and Sexton was extremely impressed with his organisation, an exclusive correspondent relationship was agreed. This might have continued indefinitely had Lawry not for purely personal reasons decided to return to the US in 1966. J&H couldn't risk their book of business falling into enemy hands, so bought his firm and sent Ken Seward from Caracas to run it.

By the beginning of the 1960s, J&H had built a commanding lead over all their competitors by establishing their own network of offices in South America. Not only was this producing good profits from local business on the ground, but they were able to use their international expertise as a door-opener to attack the domestic US business. Such was the extent of decentralisation at that time that very often the first thing a parent company knew about the insurances of their South American subsidiary was when told about it by their local J&H office.

Meanwhile, US firms had been increasingly investing in the UK and continental Europe, and by the end of the 1950s Sexton had turned his attention to how J&H could provide service to their European subsidiaries. The problem was entirely different and much more complex than in South America where no brokerage firms existed and J&H had to set up their own operations. In the UK and continental Europe there were well-established and very professional brokers, and Sexton reasoned that J&H would never be able to successfully compete with them for local business. This pointed to some form of correspondent relationship, as Sexton himself described:*

In England and on the Continent, however, there were a number of very old and effective brokerage organisations and the thought of endeavouring to enter Johnson & Higgins as an independent organisation in each of the countries involved seemed foolhardy, both from the point of view of the time and capital that would be required and the fact that we would have little chance to acquire national business in competition with well-established national brokerage firms. The better route appeared to be the establishment of a correspondent relationship with a prominent firm in each country. Difficulties, however, were inherent in this approach as well, for our relationships on the Continent before and after the Second War were sketchy at best and almost without exception limited to firms where vessel insurances were involved. Such firms as Hudig in Holland, Wuppesahl in Germany and Delapalme & Boistel in Paris would not necessarily be our first choice for the handling of corporate property insurances and in fact under the *courtier jure* system in France the marine brokers were not legally permitted to handle non-marine insurances. The obvious solution, therefore, was to turn to Willis Faber† for guidance and Dick Denby, a Life Director of Willis, was assigned to work with us on the solution of our English and European property problems. The choice was not a particularly happy one. Denby was responsible for both the employee benefit and home fire departments of Willis. We had had some experience of Denby in the latter capacity as he had handled one or two American accounts located in England and promptly adopted a proprietary air toward such accounts to the extent that he resented suggestions from this side. Nevertheless, a start had to be made and

* 'J&H International Operations 1952–1972'.
† Willis Faber, J&H's longstanding London partner (see chapter 4).

in the Spring of 1959 Denby arrived in New York to review the whole subject with us. In addition to offering Willis's assistance for matters relating to American firms in England and on the Continent he also brought with him a list of firms in several Western European countries which might be used by us as correspondents, and several of these firms were in fact subsequently approached to determine their willingness to so act.

Later in that year one of our important clients, Cofra Black, entered France and established an operation near Bordeaux. Denby was asked to contact this client on our behalf and to arrange such necessary insurances as required by the local operation. The details of what subsequently transpired are unimportant. However, from our point of view we felt that Denby had failed to carry out our rather specific instructions that had been given to him. The upshot was that we had a client who was sufficiently unhappy that it prompted a letter of complaint from Elmer Jefferson to Elwyn Rhys, then Chairman of Willis.

The Chrysler Corporation about this time decentralised their international operations, establishing their international headquarters in Geneva, Switzerland. They turned to us for guidance. Al Olsen, a director in our marine cargo department, instantly saw a chance to market their cargo contract which had been a goal of his for many years. In March 1959, Lloyd Benedict, formerly an American Foreign Insurance Association (AFIA) overseas manager, joined us and started the production activities of our international network. Consequently, he too became active in convincing Chrysler to use our world-wide chain of offices. By the end of December, Messers Olsen and Benedict had travelled together to Europe and London and returned with a broker's letter of appointment to handle the entire Chrysler International account.

Partly as a result of the Cofra Black incident and from observations developing out of the Chrysler solicitation, Dick Denby, accompanied by Derek Ripley,* again visited New York in early May 1960. In Elmer Jefferson's words at the time 'It was clear that Denby was here under instructions to make any arrangements which we might think necessary for the handling of our European business and Derek Ripley instructed to furnish moral support, or, perhaps, to be present to gain an independent opinion of what the situation required.' In defence of
* Later chairman of Willis.

19

our English friends these discussions developed the fact that Willis's direct business at that time accounted for not more than fifteen per cent of their total gross income and even this relatively small percentage was handled in an atmosphere where solicitation of new business or competition among brokers was considered ungentlemanly. One rather amusing example of this attitude was the case of the English head of one of our US clients who complained that one of Willis's partners had been rude to him at a cocktail party. When approached on the subject, the partner in question said he found this difficult to understand because he distinctly remembered saying 'Good evening' to the gentleman in question. In short, the Willis organisation, and other English brokerage houses, had not been trained in the sense of urgency required to handle direct business.

So even at this early stage, it became apparent that ways of handling business were very different in the US and the UK, and the first transatlantic complaint on servicing international business had been recorded. Sexton went on:

In addition, all of us were feeling our way as how best to handle American concerns abroad, both those which were involved in doing business in a single foreign country and those which were multinational in character with branches in two or more of the European countries. Varying regulations in the several countries regarding the requirement for local insurance in local currencies versus non-admitted insurance* in dollars were a serious problem, and various solutions were proposed . . .

The concrete result of the meetings with Denby and Ripley was an agreement that we were both in a learning period, and that it might be advisable for each firm to send a young man for several weeks' training in the office of the other so that each could become better acquainted not only with the individuals but the systems and problems as respects this class of business.

The lucky young men in question were Peter Bickett of J&H and Michael Day of Willis, who spent some six weeks in London and New York respectively in the Autumn of 1960, with the vis-

* An insurance placement that was not legal in the territory concerned.

its overlapping so they could spend time together in each office. And so began one of the key elements of international training: overseas secondments and exchanges. But back to Sexton:

Simultaneously, the 3M Corporation and the Colgate-Palmolive people indicated a growing need for more uniform overseas broker- age services. Both turned to us for answers to their problems. It was apparent from these cases, and others, that our international activity was to become quite important in the future.

In the ensuing months a strong effort was made to use our interna- tional operations as a wedge in the solicitation not only of foreign business but also the domestic coverages of US firms with foreign interests. Our strong position in South America gave us a decided edge over our competitors on that continent. However, when it came to Europe we found that that the loose correspondent relationships had decided flaws, including the fact that in some instances, in solicit- ing a new piece of business and mentioning the European corres- pondent we would use, it was discovered that the correspondent was already handling the business for another American broker. The obvious solution was to endeavour to establish a chain of correspon- dents who would act exclusively for Johnson & Higgins in a manner similar to the arrangement which had been in effect for so many years with Willis on the Marine side.

Accordingly, in the Fall of 1962 Bill Bumsted, who had returned the previous year from Venezuela and joined our board in January 1962, and Paddy Stephenson of our Montreal office and I journeyed to Europe with this purpose in mind. We recognised that the task would not be an easy one for the European brokerage firms were unused to the idea of exclusivity and in fact most of them did business with one, two, three or more brokers in the London market. We also recognised that they would feel that it would preclude the possibility of their handling important US business in their several countries where the prime broker in the US on such business was one of our competitors, and, finally, there was the question of whether sufficient business could be generated to make worthwhile the resultant necessary divi- sion of commissions. Against these probable objections we could point to the fact that we were, through our South American offices, well out in front of our American competition in the international

21

field and that only through an exclusive relationship could the mutual trust and mutual goals be established which would provide for the strongest competitive position.

By 1962, Dorrance Sexton had become president and with that post had taken on wider responsibilities, so Bill Bumsted became the first director of the international department. Paddy Stephenson went along primarily because he spoke fluent French. Sexton was heard to remark that he spoke French as fast as he spoke English, and was equally unintelligible in either.

Stephenson was an interesting man. A British national born in Dublin and educated in France, Switzerland and Belgium, he was a broker in the Room* at Lloyd's before the War. He flew Hurricanes during the Battle of Britain and famously brought down two German bombers at once by colliding with them, and managed to parachute to safety with nothing more than a broken ankle and a damaged knee. He ended the War as a wing commander on the Staff of Lord Mountbatten of Burma with a DFC, the Légion d'Honneur and the Croix de Guerre. After the War he was assistant air attaché and deputy head of the UK air mission in Paris, and went on to become assistant secretary to the Joint Intelligence Committee at the Ministry of Defence in London. On leaving the RAF in 1955 he emigrated to Canada with his Canadian wife and two children, and took Canadian citizenship in 1960. Settling in Montreal, he joined the local brokerage firm of Dupuis, Parizeau, Tremblay, Limitée which was acquired by J&H Canada in 1958. Every bit the dashing fighter pilot and one of the world's great charmers, he went on to become Chairman of J&H Willis Faber in 1973, and ended his career as Chairman of J&H Ltd in Bermuda. As Sexton records:

Bill Bumsted and I set out in early September† for London where we stopped over for one day to meet Messers Denby and Ripley before proceeding on to Amsterdam and Rotterdam for meetings with Peter Mees and Kir Verbeek of Mees & zoonen. This was followed by a visit to Mülheim where we met Messers von Kottwitz and Oschi Hübener

* The open-plan area where underwriters sit to do business.
† 1962.

of Jauch & Hübener. In each case we outlined our thesis of exclusivity and in each case we met the objections we had anticipated but, happily, also in each case the two firms agreed to give the matter further thought.

Parenthetically it should be mentioned that subsequently in each case the exclusive agreement was adopted subject to the understanding that there would be a limited number of exceptions, mutually agreed, on the basis of either some long-standing past relationship or some particularly compelling current reason.

Bill Bumsted then departed for Hamburg* and I for Brussels to meet Paddy Stephenson who had gone directly there to establish preliminary contact with the Belgian firm of Boels & Bégault and to see his friends at the Société Belge. Here we found a different atmosphere than in Holland and Germany for Emile Bégault, the head of Boels & Bégault, was anxious to establish a relationship with us to offset the growing ties between his main competitor, Henrijean, and Marsh & McLennan. After a successful visit in Brussels, Stephenson and I left for Paris to be joined once more by Bumsted and to meet with SGCA who had surfaced as one of the larger French firms and the one least likely to have conflicting US ties.

We had made a start on aligning a group of correspondents whom we hoped would buy our theory of exclusivity, which in fact they all did at varying subsequent dates. This nucleus was later expanded through the addition of Gil y Carvajal in Madrid and Costa Duarte & Lima in Lisbon. Italy remained as an uncovered area although during our visit to London, Willis agreed that they would endeavour to service business for us in that country as it arose.

So the stage was set. J&H realised that they had to provide service for their clients and prospective clients expanding into Europe, but the formula that had been so successful in South America wouldn't work in Europe. An exclusive network of correspondents seemed the ideal solution and this was worked on with J&H's long standing UK partner, Willis Faber.

But we're getting ahead of ourselves. Who were these leading national brokerage firms, and what were the characteristics of each of their countries which made doing business with them

* Head office of Jauch & Hübener.

at once so fascinating and challenging? It was going to be understanding their differences and building on their similarities which would lead the way to the operation of a successful network. Let's start with the Americans, because it was, after all, J&H who were the driving force behind this whole story.

3 The Americans

Everyone should go to America. From the moment your cab lurches over the Triboro Bridge and you get that first glimpse of the Manhattan skyline, there is a feeling of excitement. New York is a city where everything is magnified; the lights are brighter, the pace is quicker, the beautiful people are more stunning, the streets are dirtier, the buildings are bigger, the drinks are stronger, and the price of success and failure is greater. You may love it or you may hate it, but no way could you conceivably be bored. In a way, the streets of New York epitomise America. Everything is there to see – rich and poor, success and failure, all jumbled up together. Everyone is letting it all hang out, sometimes literally. Life goes on in the streets, twenty-four hours a day.

But what has really made America great are the millions of nameless people in the thousands of small towns across the country who go happily about their daily business: the barber, the gas pump attendant, the man running the hardware store, the baker. Many were immigrants, or the children or grandchildren of immigrants, over the last one hundred years, but all are now Americans participating in the American Dream. They want to make things better for themselves and their families. For this is the can-do society where everything is possible. The man collecting your trash today knows that next week, everything could be different.

But ironically, America's greatest strength is also its greatest weakness; the sense of optimism brings with it a touch of naivety and the belief that every problem arose this very morning and can be solved by lunch time. Incredible growth and prosperity over the last one hundred and fifty years has left Americans with the conviction that everywhere else could achieve the same result, if only they were to copy the American pattern.

At first sight there is no class system in America, other than the dollar. But it is there, if you know where to look. Old money, sometimes dubiously earned in the days of Prohibition, is less conspicuous than in Europe, but the privileges that go with it are just as jealously guarded.

To the visitor from Europe, the very size of the country is intimidating. New York and San Francisco don't look that far apart on the map. But here is a country that stretches from Scandinavia to North Africa and from Spain to Iran, and shows every bit as much diversity. The journey from New York to San Francisco is as far as from London to New York, and seeing the vast expanse of Nevada from 36,000 feet is like looking down on some vast sea. It is not surprising that Americans tend to be parochial and have little interest in events outside their own locality, let alone overseas. This is further encouraged by the news media. There are no national newspapers, and even the quality broadsheets have very restricted overseas news. News bulletins focus almost exclusively on local news, much to the frustration of international visitors.

But Americans have that wonderful sense of optimism and a seemingly boundless energy to try and succeed. This, coupled with a directness and genuine friendliness, makes it a wonderful country in which to do business.

Henry Ward Johnson and Andrew Foster Higgins started their firm of average adjusters in New York in 1845. They both became leading members of their profession, and by the end of the century, the firm of Johnson and Higgins had developed to become the most important marine broker in the USA. But of all the relationships that were forged in the first fifty years of the firm's existence, the one that was to set J&H apart from all other US brokers and prove to be a cornerstone in the eventual setting-up of the future UNISON network was the relationship with Willis Faber.

In the years after the Civil War, marine hull business increasingly gravitated to London, which had emerged as the most important world insurance market, and it was imperative that J&H have a means of placing business there. This they did through the long-forgotten firm of John D. Tyson & Co. of Liverpool, and their London agents, a Lloyd's broker called George Tyser. One of J&H's older clients, the Erie & Western Transportation Company, had long been on the hit-list of one

26

Thomas C. Chubb, for his firm Wreaks & Chubb. Chubb enlisted the help of his old friend Edwin Spencer, a partner in the London brokerage firm of Henry Willis & Co., and Spencer somehow managed to place the business in the London company market at cheaper rates than Tyser had been able to obtain at Lloyd's. Chubb subsequently left the brokerage to set up Chubb & Sons, underwriters, and Wreaks took his head clerk Stephen Loines into partnership as Wreaks & Loines. After Wreaks died in 1891, the firm was absorbed by J&H, probably to get the steamship account back again, and Stephen Loines set about a plan to greatly distinguish Henry Willis & Co. in the eyes of his new partners. This he achieved by winning the most important American fleet that J&H did not then control, the American Line, which Edwin Spencer succeeded in placing in the London company market with substantial backing from his foreign reinsurance* friends. J&H were suitably impressed, and rewarded Henry Willis & Co. with increasing amounts of marine business. As so often happens in the insurance brokerage business, Spencer, in his own words, had made Willis's commission 'intentionally bare' to win that first account, and subsequently wanted to readjust it. J&H sent one of their senior directors, John Barrett, and Loines over to negotiate.

Edwin Spencer in his *Recollections of a Business Life*, which he originally printed privately in 1925 for the benefit of his son John, gives amusing thumb-nail sketches of both Barrett and Loines. The former 'was a man of good looks and good manners and eclectic in his talk and enthusiasms; words flowed from him in an almost unceasing stream, and when he paused for breath, it was his habit to recommence with "Now, I am a man of few words".' Loines he describes as 'a man of fine character, a great red-bearded New England Quaker, of strong intellect, an interesting and witty talker, and with the most genial manner and the kindest heart. He regarded the best champagne and cigars, underdone beef and the game of poker as the prime necessities of life, and indulged in them accord-

* The practice of laying off part of a risk with other insurers, known as reinsurers.

ingly; but when he went out of business he retired to the shores of Lake George as a teetotaller and vegetarian, and devoted himself to the study of astronomy.'

There then took place the now famous meeting at Southampton in 1892. Barrett and Loines arrived on the *St Paul* on a Wednesday, and were due to set sail on the return journey on the Saturday. David Willis, the chairman of Henry Willis & Co., and Edwin Spencer took rooms in a local hotel, where the discussions took place. These appeared to be leading nowhere, until the very last morning. In Spencer's own words: 'Barrett, after an avalanche of jokes, most unexpectedly agreed to accept our terms; but we continued talking from the breakfast table to his cabin on board the steamer, and then backwards and forwards on the gangway, until he was pushed back to the deck of the steamer and I on to the quay, and we shouted to each other in the distance as the steamer got under way.'

Thus began the longest transatlantic insurance business relationship of all time, which was to last for ninety-eight years. It was forged by people who liked and respected each other, representing two firms that, although from opposite sides of the Atlantic, were to prove to have more in common than they could have ever imagined. The volume of business increased until J&H was sending virtually all its marine business to Willis. With David Willis withdrawing more and more from the business, this fell squarely on Edwin Spencer's shoulders, and J&H became increasingly concerned that he would end up in either the churchyard or a nursing home. At their insistence, he explored the possibility of merging with another firm, and because of Willis's leading position with London company underwriters, he wisely selected the leading Lloyd's broker, Faber Brothers. And so in 1898 was formed the firm of Willis, Faber & Co., which almost at a stroke became the leading marine broker in London.

In September 1898, Edwin Spencer and Arthur Allan, a fellow-partner who had joined from Faber Brothers, sailed to New York to further strengthen the ties with J&H and returned at the end of October with the surprising proposal from the Americans that there should be a complete amalgamation between the two firms.* But the Willis Faber partners got cold feet; after all, their own merger had only been completed ten months before. So the first of many attempts to merge the two firms came to nothing. But as a result of this meeting, J&H transferred their entire marine account to Willis, and in a gentlemanly act typical of the age, John Tyson was paid compensation for a period of five years for loss of business.

John Barrett, who the month before had become president of J&H, and Stephen Loines, now a director, once again set sail for Southampton in December 1900 and once more were met by David Willis and Edwin Spencer. From these meetings came the now historic exclusive agreement that was to be the basis of the relationship between J&H and Willis Faber for years to come. In essence, Willis was to refuse all American marine business from sources other than J&H unless specially agreed in each instance. As J&H had already promised in April 1899 to use no other English broker than Willis, the seal on the exclusive relationship was set. As everyone knows, this was a purely oral agreement, although it was confirmed in a letter from Stephen Loines once it had been ratified by the J&H Board. Many people wonder whether this agreement stretched to other lines, but in 1900, to all intents and purposes, marine business *was* the business.

This exclusive agreement came under its greatest strain with what became known as the Willcox incident. In 1923, J&H planned to merge with Willcox, Peck & Hughes, but the success of the deal was dependent on maintaining Willcox's London correspondent, C. T. Bowring, which just happened to be Willis's strongest competitor. The long-serving J&H chairman, W. Harvel LaBoyteaux (who actually died in office in 1947, having been CEO since 1916), wrote to Willis to ask their blessing. Willis refused. LaBoyteaux promptly sailed for London to argue his case and was again refused. He then told the Willis board point-blank that unless they agreed, J&H would go ahead anyway, and he would tear up the Southampton agreement. Reluctantly, Willis conceded.

The upshot of all this was that LaBoyteaux finally aban-

* 'Firm Foundations, the Origins of Willis Faber.'

doned numerous attempts over the years to put the Southampton agreement into a written contract, but produced instead a one-page memo which he called 'the idea of the agreement as it was intended'.

This contained four points:

1. The arrangement was exclusive.
2. Either party was free to cancel it at any time.
3. Neither party was to depart from the agreement without consulting the other.
4. Neither party was to circumvent the agreement to secure new business or a new market.

This last was added as a result of the Willcox incident.

By the time of Sexton's visit to Europe with Bumsted and Stephenson in 1962, the characteristics of the modern J&H had been set, and the extraordinary array of characters that was to make up the international department had begun to be assembled. Being a private company, the business was ruled totally by the directors, of whom the rest of the firm were in considerable awe. Not only were they all extremely wealthy men, as being a director of J&H had long been one of the best meal-tickets on Wall Street, but they were almost all larger-than-life characters. The by-laws had been set up in such a way that all the shares were held by the directors, and could only be passed on to those active in the firm. On election, every director signed an undated letter of resignation. When that letter was dated for whatever reason, the retiring director continued to receive a share of the profits for a period of ten years. This in itself posed a considerable deterrent to any unwelcome solicitation. The advertising of the day boasted 'We have no external shareholders – they're all inside working.'

J&H stood for professionalism, excellence and, above all, client service. The client really did come first. And thanks to Dick Purnell, who went on to succeed Dorrance Sexton as CEO in 1972, there was always tremendous emphasis on involvement in the local community. Every branch director was expected to be heavily involved with his area (there were no female branch directors).

There was tremendous emphasis on specialisation – it was seen as a way to get ahead. This was often viewed with considerable amazement by both international client and broker alike, when it meant J&H fielding a cast of thousands for any meeting. It was often discovered, after a domestic specialist was scheduled to go to London for a presentation in two days' time, that he didn't have a passport – much to the amusement of Willis Faber. Above all, there was an emphasis on production, slightly to the mystification of the brokers in Europe, to whom selling was something only done by door-to-door salesmen trying to off-load cleaning products. The need to bring in new business was ingrained into every member of the firm. J&H-ers were immediately recognisable at any insurance meeting around the country: clean-shaven, white button-down shirt, yellow tie, polished shoes and sensible suit. As often as not they would be on the speaker's platform, or at the very least in the front two rows. There was an earnestness about them, a professionalism. They knew they were better than their competitors, and so did their clients. There was almost an ingrained belief that J&H stood apart, and indeed they did.

The first full-time international employee was a far cry from the blunt globe-trotting breed that were to follow, fearlessly planting the J&H flag on often hostile parts of the globe. Peter Bickett began his J&H career at the age of sixteen as a summer intern. This continued for several summers until he became a permanent employee in the property department in 1954, after graduation from Lehigh University and a tour as an air force officer in Germany. Polished, urbane and extremely bright, he volunteered to work on the coordination of the General Motors property account, seeing this as an opportunity to get ahead. This led to joining the foreign section, the forerunner of the international department. It was Bickett who was selected to go to Willis on the first international exchange in 1960, and he and his wife Mickey sailed over on the *United States*. They lived for six weeks in a flat above the Mirabelle restaurant in Curzon Street, and worked with Michael Day under the strict tutelage of Dick Denby. Michael was then to return with his wife on a reciprocal visit to New York.

Peter was to go on in 1966 to be a roving J&H ambassador based in Milan, before Emile Bégault persuaded Dorrance Sexton to have him transferred to Brussels in early 1967. This was at the time of a huge influx of American investment as everyone got very over-excited in the early days of the European Common Market. Here Bickett got to know well the senior people in all the European correspondents,* and earn their respect. A very private family man, he was not a good traveller, and was never happier than when he returned to New York in 1968 to take over the running of some of the largest accounts of the day. After he became manager in 1970, his excellent organisational skills became the rock on which the future UNISON network was built, and he developed the system for strict control of international accounts that was the basis of quality control. Despite his reluctance to travel, he developed an excellent rapport with the Europeans and an understanding of their markets, problems and needs. He exerted strong control over the international machine and was legendary in his mastery of facts and figures. It wasn't for nothing that the wags in the marine department called him 'Peter Pentagon' (rather like English public school boys, they had a nickname for everyone, including an attractive female trainee who was known as 'Breakfast'). He sat in the train every night on his way back to New Jersey, reading through the copy telexes which in those days were still the principal method of communicating overseas. Ian Macalpine-Leny discovered this shortly after his arrival in New York. On learning that his boss, Adrian Gregory, had just been put on the Willis main board, he telexed 'Congratulations on being elected to the peerage.' Bickett came in the next morning and asked, 'What's all this about Adrian joining the House of Lords?'

In the 1960s, when a telephone speaker attachment was still quite a novelty, Peter used to relish gathering two or more of his people in his office, hooking on his speaker, and having a discussion with a network colleague in Europe. It was quite impressive in those days. On one occasion, when all had gathered in his office, the number had been dialled and connected

* As the members of the European network were then called.

32

and he went to switch on the speaker . . . a string of expletives emerged (and he never swore). The speaker was missing – it had been stolen.

If Peter Bickett was the rock on which UNISON was founded, Lloyd Benedict embodied its spirit. When he joined J&H on 1 March 1959, he already had considerable international experience. Starting with AFIA in 1946, he spent six years in Sao Paolo before becoming their country manager in Bogotá for five years. Large, gruff, and an inveterate traveller, he was the complete antithesis of Bickett, but they succeeded in forming a successful working partnership. He knew his business and, working with Al Olsen, the marine cargo director, was successful in winning Chrysler International, J&H's first international account. Colgate-Palmolive and 3M were soon to follow.

Ken Seward, who joined in the summer of 1959, was brought up to be an internationalist. His father worked for Remington Rand and he lived in Cuba from the age of nine until he was twelve. After his graduate degree from Thunderbird he joined Monsanto in their international department and ended up in New York, but he always wanted to go overseas. One day he spotted an ad in the *New York Times*: 'Young man for Venezuela, dollars hi'.* On visiting the employment agency the next day, he was told that this was for Johnson & Higgins. 'What are they?' Learning that they were insurance brokers, Ken made for the door, and was only stopped by his persuasive interviewer, who reminded him that he had taken the day off work, and as J&H were just down the street, he might as well go for the interview. Five minutes after meeting the personnel lady, he was in Dorrance Sexton's office, and the rest is history. Seward was to spend the first twenty years of his J&H career overseas. After six months' training in New York he was sent to Maracaibo, and then to Caracas. When J&H bought Gordon Lawry's business in Colombia in 1966, he became country manager in Bogotá, where he stayed until taking over in Milan in 1973. He was one of those early entrepreneurs, in the days before coordinated insurance programmes, who literally had to make it up as they went along. And provided they

* They weren't.

33

C'EST **MOI** LE PRESIDENT!

To Ken, from BARCA tw. 89

Ken Seward

turned in a profit at the end of the year, New York left them to get on with it.

Another of the great characters of the early days of the New York international department was Paul Pinkham. Having been thrown out of Cuba by Castro in 1960, Pinkham found himself in the New York property department, but soon joined the fledgling international department. His years in Cuba had left him with a penchant for Cuban cigars, which he insisted on

34

smoking in the office. What really annoyed Peter Bickett as he saw him through his glass-fronted office down the long executive corridor of the international department was not that he always had his feet on his desk, but that he had holes in his shoes.

It was customary for those with a regional responsibility to offer help to any of the account managers when going on an overseas trip. One day a circular note came round from Paul: 'I shall be visiting Lima, Santiago, and Buenos Aires. Please let me know if I can do anything for you when I am there.' Not having any Latin American responsibility, and therefore no clients there, Ian Macalpine-Leny wrote: 'Please buy me a little white sun hat size seven'. Pinkham came steaming out of his office, cigar in hand, eyes bulging, and his complexion an ominous reddish colour under his tanned skin.

There were plenty of characters on the domestic side. In the 1960s there was a heavy bias towards Princeton graduates, Sexton, Dick Henshaw, Purnell, and Ed Knetzger among others. When two bright entrepreneurial Harvard graduates at John C Paige & Co., Bob Cameron and George Shattuck, discovered that, with three young partners ahead of them, they were going to be in a nursing home before they got a share of the action, they decided to try and get an interview with J&H. This took a bit of doing, and Cameron subsequently discovered that the director who interviewed him in his Boston hotel room only did so in the mistaken belief that he was the nephew of a friend of his. After considerable delay and a lot of phone calls to New York, they eventually got an interview with Sexton. This went extremely well, in part because whenever Sexton asked 'Do you know so and so?', referring to some prominent Boston businessman, Shattuck said, 'Oh yes, I played bridge with him only last night', though Cameron knew that he had never even met him. It was agreed that Cameron and Shattuck would open an office in Boston for J&H as soon as they could extricate themselves from Paige & Co. On leaving Sexton's office, Bob Cameron was handed a telephone message from Paige; they had discovered what was going on, and both were fired. Cameron paused in the J&H lobby to call up Dorrance Sexton and announce that they had just opened the Boston office. This was in 1963.

Although the power and influence of the marine department was already waning, it carried more than its fair share of hard-working, hard-drinking eccentrics. One of the brightest, and thirstiest, was George Holloway. Holloway was extremely well read, a great anglophile, and would have gone far in J&H if he hadn't spent quite so much time in the Chateau Bar & Grill across from the office. He had a wonderful sense of humour and was the most engaging company. In the early days of the Boston office, George went up to help Bob Cameron with a marine cargo account:

CAMERON: 'Where are you staying?'

HOLLOWAY: 'The Ritz Carlton.'

CAMERON: 'But that's where Dorrance stays.'

HOLLOWAY: 'I should hope so!'

Both Cameron and Shattuck went on to become directors, but Holloway was eventually pushed out of J&H and joined Alexander & Alexander. After surviving two heart attacks and four strokes in the space of a week, George had to have a leg amputated. Paralysed down one side and no longer able to read, he somehow managed to keep his sense of humour. 'I've never believed in reincarnation,' he said, 'but the closer it gets, I might just reconsider.'

Great people, strong leadership, professionalism, and pride in their private ownership were the hallmarks of J&H. But it was the dedication to client service that ensured that J&H stood apart from their US competitors. Once they had begun to work with the leading independent brokers in Europe, market leadership in international client servicing quickly followed.

4 The British

Once he has got over how quaint everything is, no ice, and driving on the wrong side of the road, the American visiting the UK for the first time is left bemused at how small the whole place is. How could a country a third the size of the State of Texas and with a gross national product struggling to keep pace with that of California once have dominated the World? How could the British have exported their system of government, their legal system, their education, their sports and recreations, not to mention their language, world-wide? The answers are complex. The British have always been great inventors and great explorers; despite being masters of the famous understatement they also have, or had, a self-confidence that was secretly envied through out the world. In the late 18th century, there weren't the opportunities at home for impoverished second sons, or sons of the middle class, so they went overseas, to India, to the Far East, to Australasia, to seek their fortunes. But there was something else, something immediately noticeable to everyone visiting the UK for the first time, that made generations of Brits only too anxious to go overseas: the weather.

Whatever anyone may say, the weather is the only real problem in the UK, and as Mark Twain famously remarked, everyone grumbles about it, but no one does anything about it. But the weather is responsible for that most wonderful thing about the UK, which is missed by the thousands of tourists who never leave London – the English countryside. To look down on that green patchwork of fields as the plane comes in to land at Heathrow always adds an excitement to returning home. Where else in the world can you drive for an hour and see such a rich variety of countryside and town?

Although generations of Brits have happily colonised other countries, they don't like foreigners, particularly at home. They resent the continuous pressure by immigrants to enter the UK, both legally and otherwise, to compete for scarce amenities on their overcrowded island, and only tolerate tourists because of the money they spend. This mistrust of foreigners on their home ground is encouraged by the very fact of being an island. It was always fairly easy to repel invaders until the advent of the Channel Tunnel.

Whenever anyone thinks of the British, they think of the class system, and this has been exploited by the television companies. *Brideshead Revisited, Upstairs Downstairs*, and others have helped to perpetuate knowledge of the way of life of a bygone age. But despite the huge redistribution of wealth following the imposition of death duties and then the First World War, this class system still exists. Every Brit with his wits about him immediately knows where another fits in. To quote Professor Higgins in *My Fair Lady*, 'An Englishman's way of speaking absolutely classifies him; the moment he talks he makes some other Englishman despise him.' This is lost on the average American, who is still trying to understand what the Brit said, or more likely meant, in the first place. Although in the main they use the same words, the British have a completely different way of talking from Americans, a much more circuitous way, for reasons of effect. Even more confusingly, the Americans and British apply different meanings to the same word. This was aptly illustrated to the J&H board by John Goldberg, the last representative to Willis, when he unrolled a poster from Electrolux's latest UK sales campaign which said simply, 'Nothing sucks like Electrolux'. Humour does not always successfully cross the Atlantic – in either direction.

One of the many business areas that the British instigated was the insurance of ships. Although it is an international market, the language of marine insurance thus came to be English. This began a convention that the language of international insurance was English, much to the relief of the subsequent American and British members of UNISON, who tended to employ more than their fair share of monoglots.

It seems that Henry Willis started his business on or about 1 January 1828, but there are records indicating that he was in business even earlier.* Unlike J&H, Henry Willis & Co. were originally insurance brokers and commission agents, buying and selling various materials on commission in addition to their

* 'Firm Foundations, the Origins of Willis Faber'.

insurance business. The commission business wasn't finally disposed of until 1879. With the merger with Faber Brothers in 1898, Willis Faber & Co. became the leading marine brokers in London.*

In 1899, two momentous events occurred. The first was the negotiation of the exclusive agreement with J&H (see p. 29). The second was the appointment of Willis Faber as London agents for Tokio Marine Insurance Company in Japan. These were major business coups for Willis and both were engineered by Edwin Spencer. Both were to have a strong influence on the future direction of the firm. In 1917, Taisho Marine (now Mitsui Sumitomo) also appointed Willis Faber their London reinsurance brokers. This meant that the company represented two of the most important Japanese *keiretsu*,† Mitsubishi and Mitsui, and led to the early expansion of Willis into reinsurance, a side of the business J&H avoided until much later, despite the repeated entreaties of the Willis chairman of the day, who saw that they were missing out on a great opportunity.

In 1928 came the merger with Dumas & Wylie, themselves strong marine brokers, but also involved in the relatively new business of aviation insurance. From then on Willis Faber & Dumas came to dominate marine and reinsurance broking in London.

The Willis Faber broker of the 1950s and 1960s was instantly recognisable by the semi-stiff collar, the three-piece pinstripe suit, the polished black shoes, the hat and gloves. No gentleman ever went out in London without a hat, or an umbrella if there was a chance of rain. Dressing correctly was very much part of doing business. This became the epitome of the Englishman abroad in the eyes of Western Europe. With the largest marine account in London, Willis became a byword for professionalism, and above all integrity. The Willis partners and senior brokers commanded immense respect in the Lloyd's and London company markets, and had ready access to ship owners and insurance companies needing reinsurance throughout

* Ibid.
† A group of Japanese companies linked by cross shareholdings which are reinforced by close links between their managements.

Europe. London hadn't become the leading centre of insurance by reason of geography; vision, determination and, above all, flexibility gave Lloyd's and the London insurance company market an edge that simply couldn't be found elsewhere. This was rewarded by an increasing inflow of profitable business, and the involvement of countless memorable personalities, both underwriters and brokers.

Placing business at Lloyd's with its arcane practices and old-fashioned manners always appeared a complete mystery to anyone not directly involved. The underwriters (there was only one, who had a number of deputies, for each Syndicate*) were immensely powerful, and the senior Willis brokers would all have carefully cultivated the underwriters who led† their particular risks. But behind this austere exterior (everyone is still addressed as 'sir' in the Room at Lloyd's) there was an immense amount of fun, driven by an almost schoolboy sense of humour. When the first mini-skirt was spotted among the visitors on the gallery above in the old Lloyd's building, every underwriter to a man put down his pen and made for the far end of the Room to get a better look – some of them were even down on their knees.

From the very early days, Willis Faber developed strong relationships with European brokers in the search for reinsurance business. Otto Hübener and Walter Jauch, the founders of Jauch & Hübener, first visited Willis in 1923, and such a strong relationship developed that Willis Faber & Hübener GmbH was set up in Berlin in 1927 to develop international reinsurance business. Needless to say, this joint company didn't survive World War II. But the principle of reciprocal training visits was established at a very early stage between the two companies – something that was to be used to such good effect by UNISON. The relationships which were eventually to lead to the J&H correspondent network in Europe had begun to be formed.

* A Lloyd's Syndicate is a group of underwriting members of Lloyd's who are bound by the signature of an active underwriter on their behalf.
† The lead underwriter was the first to put his line, expressed as a percentage, down on the underwriting slip. If he was an acknowledged leader on that class of risk, and wrote a significant percentage, other underwriters would follow with their lines until the slip was completed one hundred per cent.

Willis went through strong growth on the non-marine side in the UK in the 1930s, leading to considerable expansion of the extensive branch network after the War. Willis was also the first UK broker to employ a team of surveyors (engineers, to the Americans), and this in itself was to lead to a lot of new business. But the UK non-marine side was always looked down on by the smart marine brokers, who thought their counterparts, even in London, only placed house-owners' policies. Unlike J&H, direct non-marine business still contributed a relatively small amount to group profits at the beginning of the 1960s.

When Henry Willis died in 1947, the same year incidentally as the long-serving chairman of J&H, W.H. LaBoyteaux, the legendary Raymond Dumas took over as chairman. Brilliant marine broker and quintessential English gentleman, he was the perfect mentor for the young generation of up-and-coming marine brokers such as John Prentice and Michael Bonn. He was succeeded in 1955 by another very good marine man, Elwyn Rhys, who seemed to spend most of his time shooting pheasants. He was actually shooting pheasants in Wales at the time of that important visit of Dorrance Sexton in 1962 (see p. 22). The task of dealing with Sexton fell to Lionel Broad (one of the life directors, as the partners were then called), who was most put out because no one had told him of the visit beforehand.*

In those days, only the fortunate few travelled overseas on Willis business, and it was often taken as an opportunity to engage in some extra-curricular activity. This gave rise to the now legendary advice to the young marine broker about to depart on his first overseas trip: 'Eat everything that's put in front of you, **** anything you can, and don't come back with a sun tan.' This was not only confined to overseas. The senior members of the firm would stay in their London flats during the week, entertaining clients or underwriters every night, and only return to their houses in the country and their long-suffering wives at weekends. To provide a little amusement in the meantime, John Roscoe, who ran the aviation department and was responsible for putting together the capacity to insure the

* *The Business and Battlecry*, p. 78.

new jumbo jets, a feat thought impossible at the time, instigated the Crumpet Club. When an aspiring young broker marvelled at how he could collect together quite such an attractive range of young ladies, he said it was really quite simple. Whenever he met a pretty girl at a cocktail party, he would ask her point-blank, did she or didn't she? If she walked away, he knew she didn't.*

Lionel Broad let himself in to the company flat in Whitehall Court with his key one evening, and found Derek Ripley on the sofa with his secretary, stripped to the waist. Derek hurriedly explained that he was massaging her bad back. She did actually have a bad back, but Lionel rather suspected that this was only part of the treatment that was being administered.†

Willis opened their first overseas office in Montreal in 1906, followed by an investment in South Africa in 1951. Australia came next in 1961, and New Zealand in 1967. The tremendous expansion of new offices in the 1980s was mainly reinsurance-driven. The 1960s and 1970s saw a huge increase in non-marine reinsurance, and Willis brokers travelled far and wide to win business from new national insurance companies being formed by third world countries. This involved frequent trips to emerging countries in what was then known as Black Africa, as well as throughout the Gulf and the Middle East. The rule in those days was that you could only travel first class if the journey was longer than four hours. This came to be challenged by one young broker who on a short flight in the Gulf found himself sitting next to a sheikh with a falcon on his fist. On two occasions during the flight the falcon lifted its tail and did what came naturally, all over the wretched chap's light-weight suit.

The 1960s and 1970s also saw a significant increase in visitors to Willis. An important factor in this was the rise in casualty business placed at Lloyd's in the 1970s, and as a result there was hardly a week when someone from J&H wasn't in Willis's London office. Prescott S. Bush, who headed up J&H's aviation department (and whose younger brother and nephew

* The aspiring young broker in question said he would deny this story if he was quoted.
† *The Business and Battlecry,* p. 66.

both went on to become President of the United States) was a frequent visitor, as was Richard A. Mittnacht, the marine director who became very close to John Prentice. It was Dick Mittnacht who developed the deadly broking technique of flatly refusing to leave London until he had achieved what he wanted. The problem with this was that it involved buying him dinner every night, and dinner was invariably preceded by a minimum of six large dry Martinis. After the third he tended to become combative and, some would say, impossible after six, until he could be enticed into a night club where there were other distractions.*

In addition to the J&H-ers, there was a never-ending stream of American risk managers, who regarded their annual visit to London for their casualty renewal, often with their wives in tow, as one of the perks of the business. Willis became very adept at spinning out what in the normal course of events would have been two meetings, plus a dinner with the underwriters the night before, to fill four days. This involved the help of the faithful band of Willis chauffeurs who did endless tours round the Cotswolds, as well as becoming a virtual extension of the broking team by passing on useful snippets of information overheard in the back seats of their cars.

All urgent communications overseas were originally done by cable and later by telex, the most important thing being the name at the end of the telex. When Jan Thesiger, who was Willis's expert on American marine liability insurance, succeeded his father as third Viscount and fifth Baron Chelmsford, he started to sign his telexes 'Chelmsford' instead of 'Thesiger'. This provoked an angry response from J&H in California which read: 'Blank Shipping Lines liabilities unable understand why Thesiger not handling with consequent unsatisfactory results stop please reinstate immediately'.† His great-grandfather, the second Baron Chelmsford, it will be remembered, had the misfortune to lose a third of the British army in Southern Africa in an afternoon against the Zulus at the battle of Isandhlwana in 1879.

* Ibid., p. 117.
† Ibid., p. 36.

When Elwyn Rhys retired at the end of 1965, Derek Ripley became chairman. Derek got on very well with J&H, in particular with Dorrance Sexton and Dick Henshaw, and even allowed Sexton to do speed trials round Berkeley Square in his Bentley. Alas for the relationship between Willis and J&H, Derek Ripley died suddenly from a heart attack while on holiday in the south of France. He was fifty-six and had been chairman for little more than eighteen months. This was to change the direction of Willis Faber. After a period when J&H and Willis were getting ever closer, they started to move apart again.

Willis was left with a problem, which was solved by making John Roscoe chairman, the first non-marine man ever to hold the position. Although Roscoe was a brilliant broker and a good chairman, he did have his weaknesses. The most important was that the management of J&H did not appreciate his somewhat liberal approach to certain aspects of his private life. He was also rather apt to have too much to drink from time to time, and become indiscreet.* On one of his first visits to New York after becoming chairman there was a big lunch for the Chubb Insurance Company at the India House, with speeches. John Roscoe in good post-prandial form was witty, but must have sailed rather too close to the wind and probably included a raunchy story or two. When he got back to London, there on his desk was a fairly stiff letter of complaint from Dorrance Sexton, who hadn't even been at the lunch.† It took a long time for relations between Willis and J&H to recover. John Roscoe retired early, at the end of 1971, following the tragic death of his companion of several years in a car crash. He subsequently married a lady of twenty-seven. John Prentice and Konrad von Kottwitz, former senior partner of Jauch & Hübener, were joint best men.

Roscoe was succeeded by Julian Faber. Julian was the son of Alfred Faber, one of the eight original partners of Willis Faber & Co. when it was formed in 1897. Educated at Winchester and Trinity College, Cambridge, he served as a major in the Welsh Guards during the war and married a daughter of Harold Macmillan, British Prime Minister in the late 1950s and early

* Ibid., p. 86.
† Ibid., p. 88.

1960s. He always appeared rather aloof, not helped by a certain shyness, but he was an excellent chairman and steered the firm through some major events: the move in 1974 to the country head office in Ipswich – a stunning modern building designed by Norman Foster; the flotation on the Stock Exchange in 1976, which was to have far-reaching implications for the relationship with J&H (see p. 163); and the acquisition of Ten Trinity Square, also in 1976. Willis finally moved from 54 Leadenhall Street, its head office and centre of operations for fifty-four years, in 1977.

The acquisition of Ten Trinity Square was something of a coup. Designed by Sir Edwin Cooper (the architect of the 1928 Lloyd's building) as the headquarters of the Port of London Authority and opened by David Lloyd George, the then British Prime Minister, in 1922, it was bought for a song from the receiver of a bankrupt property company. Willis moved in with due pomp and ceremony. The old panelled board room was just a bit short of the length of a cricket pitch, which the London insurance market felt very appropriate for such a blue-blooded broker. Ten Trinity Square was designed to impress, and impress it did. Every tourist who dared to venture into the foyer to ask the uniformed commissionaires whether this was part of the British Museum was disappointed to learn that it was just an office building. No client or underwriter could fail to notice the magnificent panelled rooms on the second floor. Willis didn't only buy the freehold of the building. The acquisition included several acres of carpet (valued at a million pounds), and Jack Burchett, the commissionaire on the front desk, who very much regarded the entire building as his own. Another great character of that time was Tom, a lovely old chap, whose sole job appeared to be to clean Julian Faber's shoes.

Once the move had been completed, Julian Faber gave a cocktail party for the London market in what came to be known as the Tower Room, which was organised by Michael Day, assisted for some reason by Ian Macalpine-Leny. Ian went down to check on the room the day before, to find two men in blue overalls winding down the two giant crystal chandeliers to take them away and clean them. He doesn't know to this day whether they were cleaning them or stealing them, but they wound them back pretty smartly.

One of the great innovations of the new building was a very substantial catering operation that could feed all the staff, in addition to three private dining rooms supplied from a separate kitchen, and the famous open plan Green Room, which catered for the majority of the business entertaining. Julian Faber had fairly firm views on how these facilities were to be used. No one was allowed to have a sandwich at their desk – this might encourage mice (it was rumoured that there had been more mice than employees in 54 Leadenhall Street) – and on no account was anyone allowed to remove his jacket in the Green Room. Unfortunately, the first person he went over to remind of this rule turned out to be a client. Walking down the executive floor one day at 54 Leadenhall Street, Julian Faber came across a chap with long hair, a particular dislike of his, loitering with the messengers. Taking a ten-pound note out of his pocket, he told him to go and get his hair cut. The man was delighted – he worked for the Post Office, who were in charge of the Willis telephone system in those days.

After he retired at the end of 1977 and Ronnie Taylor had taken over as chairman, Julian Faber retained an office in Ten Trinity Square. This allowed him to park in one of about sixteen hallowed spaces along the side of the building. Entry was controlled by a barrier and you had to speak to one of the commissionaires via an intercom to get it raised. One day as Julian arrived in his powerful car behind a delivery van, he thought that if he put his foot down he could just squeeze in before the barrier came down again. The end result was he wrote off three parked cars (one of which was brand-new, awaiting collection) and seriously damaged his own. Extricating himself from the wreckage, he walked calmly in through the front door and gave his keys to Jack, the commissionaire, saying, 'Just sort it out for me please, Jack. If you need me, I'll be in my office.' He did have style.

When Dorrance Sexton set out on his mission to put together a network of correspondent firms in Europe, it was only natural that it would be Willis to whom he would turn for advice.

Willis knew all the major brokers and underwriters in Europe and was a byword for professionalism and integrity, but the emphasis of the two firms was very different. J&H had specialised in retail* business, initially marine, but latterly increasingly in property and casualty. Willis was essentially a wholesale† placing and reinsurance broker.‡ Up to now, the two roles fitted together perfectly. But Willis's treatment of retail business was a bit of a muddle. Incoming business was handled in what was then called the home department under Dick Denby, but anything that looked as though it might have overseas subsidiaries was looked after in a special section of one of the wholesale placing departments. If the organisation was difficult to understand from outside the firm, it was often equally difficult from inside.

Dick Denby enjoyed French food and wine, as did the overseas manager of the Northern Insurance Company (later part of Commercial Union) Dennis Hawkins, and between them they had put together a very early property damage and business interruption programme for Colgate-Palmolive in France and Germany, a client Willis had looked after for some years. This formed the pattern for the early accounts, with the casualty and other business (what Denby called the 'bits and pieces') being left to its own devices.

As other accounts started to arrive, including Chrysler International and 3M, Denby transferred a young account executive called Michael Day away from purely UK clients to do the legwork in Europe. Michael had joined Willis in 1955, was a former Scots Guards officer and had an American wife, so was considered eminently suitable. He set off round Europe armed with his schoolboy French to arrange local servicing through Willis's broker friends in the various countries. The main criterion in each case was, of course, to find someone who spoke English.

Dany Kervyn readily fitted the bill in Boels & Bégault, and Santi Gil de Biedma in Gil y Carvajal. Where no suitable broker

* Insurance business placed directly on behalf of the original insured.
† Business placed on behalf of the retail broker.
‡ Business placed on behalf of an insurer with another insurer, called a reinsurer.

could be found, as in Italy and Scandinavia, Willis fell back on the local agents of the Northern. So in a sense, Michael Day was the forerunner of not only UNISON but the J&H European correspondent network as well, servicing the property damage and business interruption programmes for the European subsidiaries of American companies that were insured by early pan-European policies placed in London.

Apart from being extremely good company, Michael Day could always be singled out because his hair had gone almost completely white when he was still in his forties. Coming back from one of his European trips, the chap in the next seat on the plane asked him how he was enjoying retirement. Michael meekly answered 'Very much' and went on with his paper.

All this was to change as J&H started to win new business by putting together international programmes placed in America. Willis too started to get their act together. A former Grenadier Guards officer, Ronnie Taylor, was hired in 1959 to run the life and pensions department. After Denby died, Ronnie took over the home department in 1965, and started an extremely successful sales double act with Tommy Thomson, an excellent property and business interruption technician who had joined Willis just before the war. They were later joined by Adrian Gregory whom Ronnie brought in from Minets in 1968. These three went on to make Willis the leading broker in the UK for multinational clients.

David Palmer, yet another former Guards officer, who had run Edward Lumley's office in New York for six years, also joined in 1959. J&H tried to hire him, but when David said that he wanted to return to the UK, they gave his name to Willis and hired Lloyd Benedict instead. Even by the beginning of the 1980s, the retail side of Willis was still considered the poor relation by the rest of the group. In 1984 David Palmer, now chairman, invited Sir Kenneth Bond to lunch. Bond was finance director of GEC, then the largest client of Willis retail in the UK. He was extremely bright, formidable, and had a reputation for not suffering fools gladly. The Willis team at lunch consisted of David Palmer, John Prentice and Ken Childs (both deputy chairmen), Adrian Gregory who led the UK retail company, and

Michael Claydon. The latter was a late addition to the team in case the distinguished guest should have the bad grace to ask a question about his insurance programme. Claydon arrived early in the Red Room, the partners' dining room, suit pressed and shoes shining. John Prentice was already ensconced on the sofa, pink gin in hand. They had never met. Claydon found Prentice charming, and was immediately put at ease. When asked how long he had been at Willis, Claydon replied that he had spent twenty-two years in the retail company. 'Bad luck,' came the response.

Before leaving Willis, we should go back to the last chapter of Edwin Spencer's *Recollections of My Business Life*, entitled 'Conditions Making for Success', written for the benefit of his son, John. This is a digression from our story, but excellent advice for anyone starting off in business.

It is essential to success to have character, to be interested and keen, and to try to do your best. It is your duty in life to put something back into the world in return for what you take out of it.

As well as getting an understanding of the business, get an understanding of men; there is much of human nature in this business.

Strive to be ever cheerful in your manner; people turn to those that laugh as flowers turn to the sun.

Be wise in your choice of friends; a man is judged by the company he keeps.

And above all be careful of your health, for upon this depends the quality of your judgement and your work.

In looking back on my own intense struggles and anxieties, mixed with disappointments and failures, and then upon the successes which followed, I think I seldom won by being cleverer than others, but by trying harder. You will be starting so much later in life than I did and in a bigger field of action, but you will be equipped with many greater advantages which were denied to me, and will in good time be able to get abreast of what is required of you and then win your opportunities. Afterwards I have every confidence that where I succeeded, you will not fail; but whatever your success, you will have to make it yourself. You have only to try your best and your work will reward you; and remember this always: WHAT WE THINK, OR WHAT

49

WE KNOW, OR WHAT WE BELIEVE IS IN THE END OF LITTLE CONSE-
QUENCE. THE ONLY THING OF CONSEQUENCE IS WHAT WE DO.

This advice is as true today as when it was first written in 1924. Unfortunately, John Spencer didn't take it. He spent far too much of his time on the roof garden of Derry & Toms* in High Street Kensington practising his putting on the clock-golf course. He was eventually pushed out of Willis in 1938, probably wrongly in the view of Julian Faber, and was killed by a sniper's bullet in Normandy in 1944 while serving with the Welsh Guards.

* A well-known London department store.

5 The Germans

Germans are different. It's not something that's easy to put a finger on. They are perfectly polite, sometimes excessively so. They have even been known to have a sense of humour. But behind it all there is a stiffness. They are very organised. Where else in the world are children only allowed to play ball games in the parks specifically set aside for ball games, and where else is it a cardinal sin to hang out washing on a Sunday? Even the houses and apartment buildings seem regimented – rather perpendicular and unforgiving. On his first trip to Mülheim, a young Willis broker was also struck by the scarcity of old buildings, and had remarked on this to his hosts before realising to his horror what he had said.

Another thing immediately noticeable to the visitor from western or southern Europe is the food. Everything seems to arrive swimming in gravy, and there is a decided lack of green vegetables. Sitting down to his first lunch and not being able to read a word of the menu, that same Willis broker made the mistake of asking his Jauch & Hübener host to recommend something particularly German. When the boiled pig's knuckle arrived, he looked at it in absolute horror, before making a valiant attempt to not only eat it, but look as though he was enjoying it. Swallowing the last slimy mouthful with considerable difficulty, he put down his knife and fork with a look of achievement – only to have the waiter take away his plate and give him the second one.

For fifty-one weeks in the year, the Germans go briskly about their daily business, models of propriety and self-restraint. Then on the Wednesday before the beginning of Lent, the entire Rhineland together with Munich and Mainz go completely berserk with the start of *Karneval*. At 11.00 a.m. the following day the women traditionally take over and begin by cutting off all the men's ties. The entire population then goes on the most monumental binge for a week, with schools, offices and public buildings closing and no work getting done. On Ash Wednesday, everyone shows up for work again and carries on as if nothing had happened.

The story of Jauch & Hübener is very much the story of Germany in the twentieth century. The firm was founded in 1919 in Hamburg by two young insurance men, Otto Hübener and Walter Jauch. The old-established Hamburg brokerage firms jealously guarded their portfolios and did not take kindly to these pushy newcomers, who advertised on trams and elevated railways in an attempt to get visibility. Otto Hübener quickly realised that the East provided the best opportunity. Once the Treaty of Rapallo in 1922 had united the two outcasts of Europe, the defeated Germans and the Communist Russians, the way was opened for Russia and Germany to do business together. Soon afterwards, Otto Hübener met a Russian in Berlin looking for reinsurance, and as a result wasted no time in sending Wilhelm Möring to Russia on the first merchant ship leaving Germany. Möring managed to reach Moscow, and was the first foreign insurance man to introduce himself personally to the Gostrakh, the state-owned insurance company that had been set up in 1921. He came away from this meeting with an order to negotiate the reinsurance of the entire Russian property portfolio, an incredible breakthrough for the young firm. This in the end came to nothing because the Gostrakh decided to retain the business themselves, but Jauch & Hübener instead were to receive an instruction to place reinsurance of the Russian marine portfolio.

Otto Hübener realised that it would be very difficult to place the Russian business without involving the London market, so in 1923, he and Walter Jauch got permission from the authorities to travel to London. Only five years after the end of the war there was still a lot of anti-German feeling in London, and two or three London brokers were visited without success. They were just about to give up in despair when purely by chance they met in the street Willi Knoop, a relative of Walter Jauch, who was a client of Willis Faber. Knoop gave them a personal introduction to George Stamp, who later became chairman of Willis. This was the first of many visits, and the beginning of the very close working relationship between the two firms. It was very timely, because later in the year, Jauch & Hübener placed twenty per cent of the Russian marine reinsurance contract with the Munich Re, and Willis placed the remaining eighty per cent in the London market. Jauch & Hübener were therefore able to renew Willis Faber's link with Russia, which had been broken in 1917 at the time of the Revolution.

This was a time of hyper-inflation in Germany. Jauch & Hüberner was able to weather the financial storm because the majority of large insurance policies were placed in foreign currency. An office had already been opened in Berlin in 1922, and another office in Vienna followed in 1927. By then the relationship with Willis was so strong that a joint reinsurance company, Willis Faber & Hübener GmbH was set up in Berlin to place the Russian reinsurance business. Jauch & Hübener was now the most important reinsurance broker in continental Europe, and Otto Hübener had emerged as the dominant and controlling partner.* But not every new initiative was to prove successful. Jauch & Hübener Inc., which was set up in New York in 1928 with the help of Marsh & McLennan, was a failure.

In 1933 Hitler became Chancellor, and in due course Jauch & Hübener had a so-called counter-intelligence officer of the SS security service assigned to the company. He had to report all incidents and the travel movements of both partners and employees to his department. Because of his cosmopolitan views and international connections, Otto Hübener was considered 'unreliable' by the new regime, and in 1934 he was arrested by the Gestapo. He was quickly released, only to be arrested again two years later. This time his home was searched and documents confiscated, and he considered leaving for South America with his family, but he didn't want to leave his firm. In 1935, the Nuremberg Laws had been announced, which effectively made Jews second-class citizens. This made it imperative that Jewish partners and staff should leave the country, which Otto Hübener achieved by transferring them overseas. A share in a broker in Milan had been taken in 1934† and offices opened in Genoa and Paris (jointly with the Regamey family)‡ in 1935.

* Walter Jauch left the partnership in 1927.
† With three offices in Italy.
‡ Société International d'Assurance.

At the beginning of 1938 the joint company with Willis Faber was wound down. Later, with the outbreak of war, all London insurance contracts were replaced by the Generali Insurance Company in Italy. It is difficult for us to understand the effect of suffering a catastrophic war. The hardship and deprivation that ensued has conveniently been forgotten, but the entire period had a dramatic effect on the history of Jauch & Hübener.

Jauch & Hübener followed the early successes of Hitler's armies by opening offices first of all in Prague, then in Brussels, Antwerp, Amsterdam and Bucharest. Madrid opened in 1942. By 1940, they were indisputably the most important broker in continental Europe. But when the tide of fortune turned, Jauch & Hübener's fortunes turned with it. One by one all the new offices were given up. But worse was to follow. Otto Hübener was arrested for a third time in December 1944, because of his efforts to help a French prisoner-of-war at the request of French business friends. Thanks to him, Lieutenant Sabatier was released from prison camp, and went to work in Jauch & Hübener's Hamburg office. However, he regularly visited Otto Hübener's house, which led to a denunciation, and he was arrested by the Gestapo. He was released, only to be arrested at the border trying to get back to France. Unfortunately he was carrying some papers from Jauch & Hübener, and Otto Hübener and his brother-in-law Ernst Möring were arrested on the grounds of helping him escape. Möring was quickly released, but the investigation into Hübener was expanded because of the suspicion of his involvement with the 20 July assassination attempt. The chief executive of the Colonia Insurance Company, Mr Haus, who had spent a lot of money trying to buy Jews back from the Nazis, tried to buy Otto Hübener his freedom, but all attempts to get him released failed. He was shot on 23 April 1945.

This marked the lowest point in the history of Jauch & Hübener. Of the extensive European network, only Vienna remained. All the German offices had been badly damaged, and the domestic business was in a shambles. And the co-founder and driving force for the first twenty-five years of the company's existence was dead. 'At the same time we have sold the

54

rest of our international organisation for next to nothing and besides, have made the firm decision never again to set up such an organisation', said Dr Remé at an employee conference.*

For many Germans, the immediate post-war period brought even greater suffering than the war, with chronic shortages of food and housing. But the Germans are hard-working and determined, and Jauch & Hübener, like Germany, was to rise from the ashes. Konrad von Kottwitz and then Ewald Lahno were to lead the company in spectacular recovery. Otto Hübener's nephew Oswald (Oschi) became a partner in 1951, and his son Harald in 1971. The relationship with Willis was re-established in 1949, when it was discovered that Willis had held all the commissions due to Jauch & Hübener under the old Russian policy in a special account, providing much-needed funds for the reconstruction of the company. Otto Hübener's pronouncement in the 1930s that 'The English will keep their word'† had come true. Just as importantly, Willis introduced Jauch & Hübener to J&H.‡ Oschi Hübener took over responsibility for international business, and particularly the relationship with J&H. Despite the misgivings of some of the partners, an office was opened in Zurich in 1967.

In 1962 a young Berliner called Christian Dahms and his friend Jürgen Grupe both spent three years in Paris and London learning about the international insurance business. Disgusted that on their return the Colonia was merely going to offer them jobs as agency supervisors in the Bavarian woods, they both looked around for something more exciting. One day Christian had a call from Grupe in Paris to say he had got a job with Jauch & Hübener in their reinsurance department. Christian had never heard of them.

Not long afterwards, Christian received a letter from his father to say that as he was now twenty-seven years old he wasn't going to support him any longer, so he had better find himself a job. Following an introduction from the Colonia, Christian was working in Willis Faber at the time, so went to see

* *Jauch & Hübener 75 Years.*
† Ibid., p. 61.
‡ Ibid., p. 62.

Derek Ripley to ask what he should do. 'Do you want to work in the UK or Germany?' came the reply. Christian thought that as he had no old school tie and no connections in the UK, he had better opt for Germany. 'Then there's only one firm you can work for,' said Ripley, 'Jauch & Hübener. I'll arrange an interview.' So on 1 May 1965, Dahms started in the direct department of Jauch & Hübener. As he was the only person in Mülheim who spoke English and French, he was soon transferred to the international department reporting to Oschi Hübener.

Christian became a protégé of Oschi, who arranged for him to go to J&H for twelve months in 1968 as a trainee. Here he was to fall under the spell of Bob Roberts, the legendary deputy manager of the New York casualty department. Roberts lived and breathed casualty insurance, but was also a great people person, and the greatest supporter of his young brokers and trainees. He would do a full day's work and then, until the small hours, be at whatever gathering of J&H-ers was happening that evening. Seven o'clock the next morning, there he'd be at his desk, fresh as a daisy, stretched back in his chair with his feet on his desk, on the phone to London. On top of all this, he managed to find time to father nine children.

Christian's time with J&H sowed the seeds of his success in business, because he learnt something that no one had told him in Germany: if you want to succeed, you have to work hard. He also developed a huge respect for J&H, their people, their way of doing business, and their professionalism. This was to make him one of the most dedicated supporters of UNISON in the future. When his stay with J&H was drawing to a close, Lloyd Benedict took him out to lunch. 'I hear you would like to stay in the US,' said Benedict. 'Well,' replied Christian, 'it had crossed my mind.' 'Oschi Hübener sent you over here,' said Benedict, 'and I'm going to send you back.' J&H had already learnt that their converts were much more effective if they returned to their own companies to spread the word. Christian was the perfect example. Indeed, many of his colleagues considered that he returned almost too immersed in the J&H philosophy.

Back in Germany, Christian took over from Hörst Hendrich

as manager of the international department and, with the full backing of Oschi, started to implement the J&H way of handling international business. Up till then, this had all been with the German subsidiaries of American clients introduced by J&H, but it was to lead on to Jauch & Hübener's first own truly international account, which ironically was British-owned.

Uni-cardan was a subsidiary of the Birfield Group, which was acquired by the major UK company Guest Keen & Nettlefolds (GKN) about 1970. The GKN insurance manager Mike Faiers thought he had better go out and take a look at Uni-cardan. Faiers was an interesting man. On leaving school in 1941 at seventeen he volunteered for the RAF and ended up training as a navigator – he couldn't be a pilot because he was too short to reach the pedals. He was then seconded to the Royal Canadian Air Force and flew a number of sorties over Germany in Halifaxes. On being demobbed, he joined the small London broker Rowbothams, ending up as managing director. Being sick of Lloyd's, he left in 1968 to become risk manager (actually insurance manager in those days) of GKN. He was a feisty little chap, very good company, but could turn ugly pretty quickly if things went wrong.

On arriving at Uni-cardan he was introduced by the company secretary to their insurance broker, Christian Dahms.* Faiers lost no time in telling Christian that this was an internal GKN meeting so he had better go back to the office, but not before he had arranged to subsequently go and meet Jauch & Hübener. 'Have you been to Germany before, Mr Faiers?' asked the Jauch & Hübener chauffeur sent to bring him back to the office. 'Yes, in 1943,' said Faiers. 'I was flying over Germany at the time dropping bombs on Düsseldorf.' The rest of the journey was spent in silence.

Despite this inauspicious start, once at Jauch & Hübener Mike Faiers was mightily impressed with Oschi Hübener and

* When Oschi Hubener learnt of Faiers' impending visit, he gave Dahms the job of researching which company was owned by GKN, and which was Jauch & Hübener's client. With a certain amount of difficulty, Dahms discovered this was Walterscheid Schmiede und Presswerk GmbH in Trier, which had been taken over by Uni-cardan.

Christian Dahms, especially when they handed him a summary of all Uni-cardan's insurances, and that of their European subsidiaries. Up to that point, Faiers didn't even know that Uni-cardan had any European subsidiaries. He was ushered in to meet the senior partner, Mr Lahno.

'*Afrika Korps,*' said Lahno, tapping his tin leg with his stick.

'RAF,' said Faiers.

'I know,' said Lahno.

Faiers subsequently invited Hübener and Dahms to a meeting at a Heathrow hotel in 1971. After lunch, all three were standing in a line in the men's room and Faiers said to Oschi, 'Jauch & Hübener will become brokers to all my companies in Germany if this guy [pointing to Christian*] becomes my account executive.' Oschi said to Christian afterwards that this type of appointment happens only once in an insurance broker's career.

Oschi Hübener was very urbane and professional and totally won over Faiers' boss Paddy Custis, the finance director of GKN. As a result Jauch & Hübener were appointed at the beginning of 1975 to arrange co-ordinated European programmes for the whole of GKN Europe, much to the chagrin of Willis Faber, who were appointed GKN's UK brokers in 1976. Mike Faiers became increasingly close to Jauch & Hübener, and good friends with Dahms and his family.

The German mentality was ideally suited to the control and co-ordination of international insurance programmes, so when Willis, who at that time were several years behind Jauch & Hübener in this area, wanted to learn, it was to Germany they turned. Adrian Gregory and Tommy Thomson came over to meet Oschi Hübener and Christian Dahms in 1976; fortunately the chemistry was good, and they all ended up the best of friends. Thomson found it difficult to understand how the chain of command would be followed through from controlling to local servicing broker, who in turn would report back to the centre. 'The trouble with you, Tommy, is you haven't met enough Germans,' said Christian. 'The trouble with me, Christian, is I've met too many bloody Germans.' Thomson had been

* It wasn't clear with what.

taken prisoner by the Italians after the fall of Tobruk, and after a year in a prisoner-of-war camp in North Africa was transferred to Germany. When the war ended he was on the Austro-Hungarian border, and had to walk home.

Jauch & Hübener was to go on to become the third largest producer of business for the UNISON network, after J&H and Willis.

6 The French

Paris is an inspiring city, and just to walk down the Champs-Elysées, or along the banks of the Seine, lifts the soul. Incredible buildings follow one after another, preserved forever from the cancer of modern developers. There is a gentleness despite the roar of the traffic; even the people walk slowly. There is an elegance; young and old alike dress as though they expect to be seen. Where else in the world are all the chairs in a pavement café arranged to face outwards? Somehow the girls seem so much prettier than in London, and everyone makes the very most of what they've got. There is an air of mystery as a hastily opened door gives a glimpse of a splendid courtyard beyond, or an elegant lady is ushered into a waiting taxi. Paris, like every city, comes into its own at night. The Arc de Triomphe looks simply stunning at the centre of L'Etoile – almost the centre of the world. And the whole city seems alive as the *bateaux-mouches* glide silently up and down the river.

The French and the English have been fighting on and off ever since the Normans first landed in 1066. It is really a love–hate relationship. The typical Frenchman likes the English – polite, stiff upper lip, etc. – but hates the country – cold, wet, awful food. The typical Englishman on the other hand loves France – warm, great countryside, wonderful food and wine – but can't stand the French. Whenever the French and the English have managed to work together, there have always been problems. The greatest technological achievement of all, Concorde, produced an unseemly wrangle as to how it should be spelt. Finally the English conceded with pretty poor grace that it should have the final 'e'. But they were to get their own back on the completion of the Channel Tunnel when the London terminus for the Eurostar became Waterloo, the site of the greatest French military defeat of all time – by the English, of course. The American view of the French has moved from mild distrust to open hostility in recent years, with, so far, little chance of a *rapprochement*.

The French make the most perfect friends and companions.

They are wonderful hosts, immensely hospitable, amusing and fun, but to do business with they can be something of a nightmare. Extremely proud and rather over-excitable, they have an uncanny knack of making everything more complicated than it needs to be.

The original firm of brokers selected by Dorrance Sexton, Société Générale de Cortiage d'Assurances, better known as SGCA, was run by Jean Claude Regamey,* who was also the principal shareholder. Regamey was the most wonderful company, a born entertainer, and an evening out with him in Paris could last till breakfast. This thoroughly suited Bob Ashton, the lawyer from Chrysler who was responsible for the company's insurance programme, but even Michael Day, who wasn't exactly naïve, often had to make an excuse and go to bed early. However, Regamey's skills off the field were not matched by his ability to control his company, and the complaints started to come in. In a determined effort to try and turn things round, J&H put one of their own international people into SGCA. In

* His father had formed SIA, the 50:50 joint venture with Jauch & Hübener (see p. 53).

To Michael Day
BARCA / Madrid. Sept. 1980-

THE FRENCH BROKER COMPLAINS TO THE LONDON UNDERWRITER OF THE SLOW SETTLEMENTS OF CLAIMS AT LLOYD'S...

the meantime Jean Claude Regamey's life style had started to catch up with him and, needing cash to sort out some domestic problems, he sold a controlling interest to J&H's competitor, Reed Stenhouse, in 1975. This gave J&H the opportunity they had been waiting for – to look for another correspondent broker – and Willis Faber came to the rescue.

Willis had been very impressed with Gras Savoye when they were both working on the Channel Tunnel feasibility project, and David Palmer arranged to introduce Dick Purnell, then Chairman of J&H, to Max Lucas, the chairman of Gras Savoye, and his son Patrick.* Purnell greatly amused the French by insisting that the meeting should not be held in Paris in case he be recognised. They met in Versailles, and the basis of an agreement was drawn up on a napkin after a very good lunch the following day. Max Lucas was a very impressive man, extremely powerful and very well respected throughout the insurance community. He didn't speak any English – but when he said '*Moi, je suis le boss,*' his meaning was pretty clear.

Gustave Gras and Pierre Savoye started their company in Lille in 1907 as brokers to the textile industry. It wasn't until the uncertain year of 1941 that the firm opened an office in Paris. Back in 1938 Max Lucas had joined as a young producer who wasn't even on the payroll. He was to go on to transform the company in the postwar revival of France. By this time the three family partners were old and not very effective, and spent so much time quarrelling that they were more like competitors than partners. Max Lucas quickly became the firm's biggest producer, and set about building Gras Savoye to be the third-largest domestic broker in France. Because of the curious structure of the partnership agreement, the partners could engage in business outside France on their own account, and Max Lucas formed an alliance with his old friend Raymond Jutheau to set up joint ventures to service business in French-speaking Africa. Needless to say they eventually fell out, and the shareholding was disbanded, but in 1965 Faugère & Jutheau were still servicing what little business Gras Savoye had in Africa.

After the obligatory training with British and American bro-

* Jauch & Hübener used Gras Savoye to service GKN in France.

kers, one of which was Willis Faber, Max's son Patrick joined in 1965. Every bit as determined as his father, good-looking, charming and the consummate politician, Patrick wanted to make Gras Savoye an international broker. There was a correspondent relationship with both Glanvill Enthoven and Sedgwick in London which hadn't produced much business, and also with Frank B. Hall of the US, but they only had one big account, Kodak. Attempts were made to start a small international network, but not much business flowed, though an office had been opened daringly in Madrid in 1965. The timing was perfect for the approach from J&H.

J&H had tried to rectify the problems with SGCA by seconding an international man to their Paris office. It was always something of a mystery how international people were selected for overseas assignments, but not in this case. SGCA was located on the boulevard Haussmann, so Lloyd Benedict arranged for E. Hugh Hausman to be transferred from Caracas to Paris in 1968. Hugh Hausman was one of the great characters of J&H international, and there are probably more stories told about him than any one else. He was an extremely good technical insurance man, which is how he first came to J&H's attention. The quintessential bachelor, he was very kind and had infinite time and patience to pass on his experience to others. He joined J&H from AFIA in Caracas in 1966, where he had recently been transferred from Manila. The first thing you noticed about Hugh was his dress, which could best be described as early 1950s. It never changed once he had come down from the University of Washington: smart, somewhat old-fashioned suit with trouser turn-ups (cuffs to the Americans), obligatory white handkerchief in the breast pocket, polished black brogues that had a welt at least half an inch wide all round the stitching giving an impression of large black polished paddles, and an old-fashioned overcoat complete with breast pocket. In winter he invariably wore a fedora,* the like of which was never seen outside the movies. He had impeccable manners which never deserted him however much the worse for wear he became, and spoke in a deliberate, slow drawl with

* Felt hat dented lengthwise, originally with curled brim.

the inevitable cigarette sometimes still between his lips.

Chip Bechtold was working for the Factory Mutual in London at the end of the 1960s and early in 1970 he thought he had better introduce himself to J&H's representative in Paris. Hugh kindly responded with an invitation to lunch, and Chip showed up at the allotted time of 12 noon. By 1.30pm Hugh was still in mid flow about the problems of introducing the concept of highly protected risks into France. Suddenly at 1.45 p.m. he looked at his watch and announced that they should go for a spot of lunch – they would go to his favourite restaurant just down the street where he went all the time. This came as somewhat of a relief to Chip, who was beginning to think that he must have made a mistake about the lunch invitation. No one seemed to know Hugh when they got to the restaurant, but they were eventually shown to a table. 'Now what would you like to drink?' he said, the moment they had sat down. 'Ah, gascon, gascon,' he said waving his napkin. Eventually a waiter appeared.

'Oui, Monsieur?'

'Ah, um, je desiré un glass . . .'

'Pardon, Monsieur?'

'Yes, un glass de . . .'

'Comment, Monsieur?' The waiter was beginning to get impatient.

'Oh, just give me a gin and tonic, damn it,' came the reply. After almost ten years in France, Hugh only managed to learn about a dozen words of French, none of which could be understood by any self-respecting Frenchman.

Once the decision had been made by J&H to change correspondent from SGCA to Gras Savoye, a decision incidentally supported by all the other European correspondents, there came the problem of transferring the J&H accounts. Already showing that ability to be one jump ahead of everyone else for which he has always been renowned, Patrick Lucas had ensured that the transfer of Hugh Hausman and two additional J&H international account executives, Paolo Carega and Luk van Berckelaer, was part of the deal. Luk van Berckelaer was a Belgian who had been working with J&H in New York, and Paolo was transferred from J&H Rome. He arrived complete with his Ferrari, which was promptly stolen, so he went out and bought another one. Everyone knew when Paolo was coming or going from the office because the Ferrari made so much noise in the underground car park that the building shook. A flamboyant character, Paolo would leave princely tips in restaurants where not even Patrick Lucas would entertain at lunch time. When renting a car for business purposes, he invariably opted for the best available model. But he was a good insurance man.

The fact that all except two of the J&H-introduced clients (one of which was Chrysler – all those nights out with Jean Claude Regamey saw to that) were subsequently transferred was very much down to the dogged professionalism and self-less determination of Hugh, who proceeded with the task in hand totally oblivious of the French. Indeed, it has always been assumed that if he had been able to understand how rude his hosts, both old and new, were being about him, he would never have been able to complete his assignment. He would march in to the office of Jacques Wagner, Gras Savoye's senior property manager and the doyen of the French property market, with Frances Cave, his translator, almost running to keep up, and tell him exactly what he expected for the clients of J&H. 'But that's not what we do for the large industrial clients of Gras Savoye,' said Jacques Wagner. 'Tell him I don't give a damn what he does for the clients of Gras Savoye,' he shouted at Frances, 'That's the way its got to be done.' Frances Cave started very diplomatically to explain in French to Mr Wagner that there was a slight problem here, but Mr Wagner looked at Hugh and Hugh looked at Mr Wagner, and the message had clearly been received.

There are endless stories of Hugh Hausman in some club with his back to the floorshow and an extremely pretty girl almost sitting in his lap, solemnly explaining to a client the finer points of sprinklers. He certainly lived the business.

In spite of the arrival of the three J&H-ers, Patrick Lucas realised that he had a problem. There was a huge influx of new business, and he simply didn't have enough English-speakers to deal with it. So he put an advertisement in the English insurance press for account executives.

One wet Thursday afternoon in Manchester, England, a

rather disconsolate Mike Barrett was looking through the job advertisements at the back of the *Post Magazine*. Everyone always read these first. And there he saw 'Account Executive – Paris'. There were only two requirements, fluent French and some knowledge of international insurance, and he had neither. But life in Manchester was pretty depressing, so he quickly decided he must be the perfect candidate, and spent the next hour composing a letter to the agency. Much to his surprise, they rang up and offered him an interview. As this meant a weekend in London, all expenses paid, he accepted with alacrity. He explained at the interview that he had only worked domestically, but international insurance must be pretty much the same; he had done French at school a few years ago and could soon brush this up in two or three weeks. When he was told the firm was Gras Savoye, he had to ask if they would please write it down.

A couple of weeks later he was on holiday and the phone rang. Would he be available for an interview in Paris in three days' time? Slightly taken aback, he thought rather hurriedly of another free weekend, this time in Paris, said yes of course, and put the phone down. Then he panicked. He went straight out and bought a French phrase book, thinking that his only hope was to learn a few phrases, so he would always have something to say in reply, whatever he was asked. Still reading his phrase book he arrived at Charles de Gaulle, and managed to explain his predicament to his taxi driver. Seeing this as an opportunity for both of them, the taxi driver spoke to him in English, and Mike answered in French. Arriving early, the taxi driver said he would buy him a coffee, thus gaining another precious twenty minutes of practice. Quaking in his boots, he presented himself at Gras Savoye's offices at the allotted hour.

Mike was interviewed by the manager of the international department, Henri Sommer. Henri was Austrian, spoke fluent French, German and English, and had been brought in by Patrick Lucas in 1973 to set up the international department. He took Mike up to meet Patrick, and then took him to lunch. And no one spoke a single word of French to him. At the very end he had a couple of minutes with the personnel manager, who had no English, but by then he had got the job. My word, he thought – these people must be desperate. Afterwards he realised he must have been the only candidate.

A couple of weeks after he started he went to Henri Sommer and said *'Henri, je départ à manger,'* using the word 'to eat' taught to every English school boy. 'Mike,' he said kindly, 'Animals *mangent* – you *déjeunez.'* That was a lesson that was never forgotten. Henri Sommer was a kind, very cultured, fastidious man who was always impeccably dressed, usually sporting a bow tie, and a beret whenever he went out. He had started his insurance career with Faugère & Jutheau in 1959, and been sent to work in both Germany and London. But that firm could not offer the international career that he wanted, and he eventually resigned.

Having to deal with Hugh Hausman did not come easily to Henri Sommer. He found in Hugh a man with whom one could discuss any subject in the world, providing it was about insurance and insurance exclusively. On one occasion they had to drive from Texas Instruments in Nice to Gillette in Annecy.* It was a fairly long trip, and Henri had chosen a particularly picturesque route, thinking it would please or even enthral his American companion. At about half way, Hugh was desperate for a cigarette, so Henri pulled into a resting place. There before them was a magnificent view over plains, river and forests, with snow-covered mountains draped in a faint bluish haze on the horizon. Birds were singing, and a gentle breeze brought the sweet scent of nearby flowers. Hugh, who up to now had paid no attention to the landscape they drove across, but kept talking at length and in great detail about the property damage and business interruption insurance programmes he had arranged in the past, got out of the car, lit the cigarette he had been craving, took a deep, deep draw, and carried on '. . . at that point I said to Jerry,† listen, you gotta increase that second layer and reduce the deductible . . . '

When Hugh Hausman was transferred to Tehran in 1978

* A journey across the Alps of between four or five hours before the motorway was built.

† Jerry Karter, who was at that time an underwriter with the Factory Mutual.

(leaving behind in his apartment five identical pairs of shoes), he was replaced by George Rainoff. If Henri found Hugh difficult, he found George impossible. But the feeling was not reciprocated. They were just two very different people doing two totally different jobs.

In the space of twelve months, the international department grew to be a tight-knit truly international group. In addition to Hugh Hausman and Henri Sommer there was Paolo Carega, Luk van Berckelaer, three Brits and two token Frenchmen – one of whom, Martine Dacla, was very much a French woman. Later they were to be joined by a Canadian and an Australian. This was absolutely revolutionary at a time when most French brokers didn't have anyone who spoke English.

J&H agreed that Gras Savoye could keep their office in Madrid provided it didn't compete with their Spanish correspondent, Gil y Carvajal, but opportunities for growth were limited. Meanwhile, clients in French-speaking Africa were still being serviced by Faugère & Jutheau, which was no longer acceptable. As J&H were perfectly happy to allow Gras Savoye to operate in countries they had never even heard of, Patrick Lucas set about opening offices there. Gabon was the first, followed by Ivory Coast and Cameroon.

In 1974 the Shah of Iran had arranged a large exhibition in Tehran, and Gras Savoye were appointed brokers. Iran had always been a target for French investment and many business people spoke French. Following this exhibition, Patrick Lucas decided to open an office in Tehran, and sent Claude Sautière out to run it. Claude was the son of a Dunkirk dentist. After qualifying as an actuary, he was hired by Max Lucas and went to work for Gras Savoye in Lille in 1968. Very ambitious, he had many of the strengths of Patrick Lucas, but wasn't quite so sure-footed. But he was immensely able, very good company, and had great strengths as a leader and motivator. Claude made a great success of the new Tehran office and on his return was replaced by Luc Malâtre. After a mere two weeks in Paris, Claude was on his way to New York to learn about J&H. He and his vivacious wife Evelyne are probably best remembered for the incredible parties they gave in New York. On his return to

Paris in 1979, it wasn't long before Henri Sommer moved to a production role, and Claude set about presiding over the enormous expansion of Gras Savoye international. This suited everyone, because Henri had believed for some time that J&H didn't trust him, and wanted to leave the international department.

Gras Savoye somehow managed to exhibit all the characteristics of the French. There were always endless problems and complications, but nothing that couldn't be resolved over a *poire* in the Café du Bois at the end of the day.

Claude Sautière

7 The Spanish

Spain – the very word conjures up a feeling of warmth: the hot sun beating down on the shoulder blades, the glow of *Rioja* with a good dinner, and the real look of mystery in the eyes of every *Señorita*. This is a country of contrasts, of the very old, and the very new, but all bound together by the genuine warmth of a people who still practise those old-fashioned manners that have sadly been swept away in much of the western world. These are a proud people, who pride themselves on standing shoulder to shoulder with family and friends. But if one of your relations stole the wife of one of theirs in 1424, that deed would be just as real today as if the last five hundred and eighty years had never passed.

To anyone other than the Spanish, the whole business of meal times is something of a mystery. They almost certainly have breakfast, but no foreign business visitor has ever caught them at it, because breakfast is a meal to be taken alone. Lunch appears anywhere between 2.30 p.m. and 3.30 p.m. and dinner at 10.00 p.m. if you are lucky. It is quite impossible to get a dinner reservation in Madrid before 9.00 p.m. at the very earliest because the waiters are still setting the tables. This tends to wreak havoc with carefully co-ordinated business itineraries put together many weeks earlier in London or New York. The one thing known about Spain the world over, the *siesta*, is claimed to be a thing of the past, but why else would the office lunch hour last from 1.30 p.m. till 4.00 p.m.?

The moment you step through the front door of 8 Mejia Lequerica, the headquarters of Gil y Carvajal in Madrid, you know you are entering somewhere very special. Pedro, the uniformed armed guard, looks you up and down before motioning you through to the large reception area manned by two young ladies who could have stepped straight from the pages of *Vogue*. Then it is up in the tiny mahogany-panelled elevator that some how manages to squeeze into the stairwell of the spiral staircase. The elevator stops with a jolt at the second floor, you extricate yourself with difficulty, two tall mahogany doors fling open, and there is the smiling Charo to lead you into the Salón Presidencia. The room seems to be filled with fresh cut flowers and the most wonderful artwork, and sofas and chairs that look as if they have never been sat on. Before you can find out, there at your side is Benito with a glass of cold *La Ina* on a silver salver. Finally your host, Santiago Gil de Biedma, chairman of Gil y Carvajal, sweeps in.

Santi is not a tall man, but he has a presence. He is impeccably dressed, and has all the manners and mannerisms of the European nobility. Close your eyes for a moment and you can see him dressed in toga and laurel leaves about to pronounce some imperial decree in ancient Rome. But beneath that slightly theatrical exterior lies a very shrewd businessman.

Gil y Carvajal was set up in 1929 by a group of prominent businessmen, including Santi's father. He was the deputy chairman of Spain's largest shipping line as well the largest Spanish shipyard. They had decided that rather than going to London to place the insurance on their ships, they would to do it themselves. They knew nothing about insurance, so they hired the marine manager of the Generali insurance company to run their new insurance broking company for them.

Santi was the youngest of three brothers. When he joined Gil y Carvajal in 1958 at the age of 22, he was the thirteenth employee and the manager was the same man who had been lured from the Generali in 1929. He immediately set about learning the business, and spent time with Hogg Robinson in London, the brokers who placed Gil y Carvajal's two marine contracts in the London market. Although the Spanish market was very rigid, Santi could see that what he had learnt in London could be adapted to Spain. This was perfect timing, because Spain was just emerging from the economic doldrums of the Franco era. Santi went to work with a vengeance and by 1963 had been made managing director because, in his own words, he was the only one in the company who spoke English.

When Michael Day arrived from Willis to find a local broker

71

to service Chrysler International, he found to his relief the English-speaking Santi, and quickly decided that Gil y Carvajal was just what was needed for Spain. By the time that J&H had got further international appointments, they discovered that Gil y Carvajal were already brokers to ITT and 3M in Spain. Santi quickly realised that here was an excellent opportunity for additional growth, and recommended to his father, who was non-executive chairman, that Gil y Carvajal should join this new network.

But there was a problem. In addition to the business from J&H and Willis, Gil y Carvajal represented Alexander & Alexander on two accounts. So Santi set off to New York for six weeks to go and meet both firms of brokers. He found Alexander & Alexander very nice, if rather old-fashioned, but he was most impressed with J&H. On being taken to meet Dorrance Sexton, he announced to the slightly bemused American (who up to then had been issuing all the invitations) that he had decided that his company was going to do business with J&H and they were going to marry Spanish style – for life. So began the relationship between J&H and Gil y Carvajal, which was to prove to be the closest in UNISON.

The problem, as far as J&H was concerned, was what would happen to Gil y Carvajal if Santi left the company? But as Santi was to explain to Bill Bumsted and Lloyd Benedict, he had two very expensive pastimes, shooting partridges and playing polo, so leaving Gil y Carvajal was not an option.

Santi's good friend Paddy Satrústegui, who became deputy chairman of Gil y Carvajal and ran operations in the north of Spain, gave Santi much support in his dealings with J&H and the future UNISON partners. His father had been another of the founders of Gil y Carvajal. Blinded by a bullet through his head during the Civil War, Ignacio Satrústegui was an amazing man who even managed to play golf. Paddy was charming, enormously enthusiastic and always the greatest supporter of UNISON.

After Santi, Paddy, and Santi's secretary, Charo, the next most important person in Gil y Carvajal was Benito. Benito did everything for Gil y Carvajal that made all the difference to the

B.
Sevilla
Mayo 93

Bob Beane

life of a Spanish gentleman. He was chauffeur, butler, cook, waiter, and loader when Santi was shooting partridges. He spoke no English, but knew immediately what any of Santi's foreign guests needed, and had it on hand.

Another early employee who was to leave his mark on the future of Gil y Carvajal was not Spanish, but American. S. Robert Beane originally joined J&H Philadelphia in 1967 as an employee benefit consultant, but left after two years to move to Spain to start his own import-export business. This didn't work out, so in September 1969 he applied for a job in Gil y Carvajal. He initially worked part time, but business was so good that he was soon on the payroll and started the employee benefit department. Eventually Santi asked him to turn it over to the people he had trained, and set up an international department with Paco Carvajal. One of the first people he hired was Javier Barcaiztegui, a young man who had originally come to Gil y Carvajal for a summer job on 1 May 1972.

Javier Barcaiztegui, the Marqués de Tabalosos in private life, is someone who has the remarkable gift of making everyone

73

seem the one person in the world that he wants to talk to. With a warm personality, an expressive face, wide smile, perfect manners, an impeccable dress sense and a wonderful sense of humour, he didn't take long to become the international face of Gil y Carvajal and a well-known figure throughout the network.

At the time when United Technologies Corp. (UTC) still had part of their business with J&H and part with Marsh, Javier had to accompany their tough American risk manager, Mike Macdonald, from Madrid to San Sebastián to visit one of his companies. This was Javier's home city and there was a good deal of celebrating going on with the end of the Franco era. The following day when they had completed their visit they went out to the little airport at Fuenterrabia to fly back to Madrid. It was winter, and terrible weather. The plane was delayed so, having already had a long Spanish lunch, they ended up in the bar. Here Javier caught sight of his old friend Antonio, who happened to be the captain of their Iberia flight back to Madrid. Javier explained that he was travelling with a very important client, and didn't want anything to go wrong.

No sooner were they strapped into their seats in the little Fokker than the stewardess came back and said to Javier that the captain needed some help flying the plane. 'My God, not again,' said Javier. 'This happens every time,' and leaving an incredulous Mike Macdonald, he disappeared into the cockpit. It was a really bumpy flight, and after about half an hour Javier appeared at the cockpit door to ask an ashen-faced Macdonald if everything was all right. Finally they landed in Madrid, and Mike was so grateful that Javier thought he was going to kiss him. It was probably entirely coincidental that not long afterwards Mike Macdonald transferred all his international business to J&H.

Javier developed a strategy of employing very bright and extremely attractive daughters of important Spanish businessmen in the international department. As with many offspring of affluent Spanish families, they had acquired part of their education abroad and had fluent English and French. These secret weapons were used to great effect on international accounts.

Spain is a country where things are still done properly and manners and breeding are considered important. Many an American who failed to thank for hospitality unwittingly earned the displeasure of his Spanish hosts. Javier Barcaiztegui had a particular dislike for the American habit of holding break-fast meetings. On being forced to attend one such meeting at Gleneagles in Scotland, he appeared at the table in silk pyjamas, silk dressing gown, and a cravat. All the Americans clapped.

That Gil y Carvajal rose from being a twelve-man broker in 1958 to the leading broker in Spain was due to the vision, drive and keen business sense of Santi Gil de Biedma. And with it came a sincerity and warmth that was to ensure Gil y Carvajal a prominent place in UNISON. Coupled with his close friendship with Bob Hatcher, this made certain that Gil y Carvajal became inextricably linked with J&H.

A not so secret weapon –
Lourdes Cuervo

8 The Italians

Italy is a land of seemingly endless variety: the Alps and lakes of the north; the canals of Venice; the art gallery that is Florence; Rome, the Eternal City, and all that it represents in the history of civilisation; the beauty of Naples and Capri; and the rugged sun-drenched South and Sicily. With every region comes a different food and a different wine, and all are equally delicious. But it is not only the landscape and the food that change from north to south. The people are equally diverse. A typical Milanese would not look out of place in Düsseldorf, while a Sicilian would be perfectly at home in Algiers. There is a love of family, of art and music, of food and wine, and of the good things in life. Most visitors remark how friendly and helpful the people are to tourists.

But in this country of contrasts, the generosity to visitors does not extend to fellow-Italians. There is intense dislike between north and south. Northerners view all southerners as lazy and dishonest, and the latter regard the former as arrogant money-grubbers. Throughout the entire country there is a deep distrust of all government – the only people who can be trusted are the family. This is the reason that Italy has been able to grow and prosper despite the seemingly endless revolving doors of successive governments in Rome in the post-war era. The people simply ignore Rome and go about their business.

In the late 1950s and early 1960s, Italy moved from being an agricultural to an industrial economy. Insurance was dominated by insurance companies and one-company agents. It was not a sophisticated market, and brokers as such did not exist.* This gave J&H the opportunity of not only following the tried and tested path of starting their own company, but at a stroke getting a toe-hold in Europe at the all-important time when the

* Many years later, an insurance company executive was to remark to Seward: 'Before the brokers came we controlled the market. We were the oysters. But you were an irritant, like a grain of sand. It has taken time, but together we have produced a pearl.'

European Community was beginning.* Switzerland was also considered, as was Brussels. The latter was heavily pushed by old Emile Bégault, who offered J&H assistance of every kind. But there was a strict no-nepotism rule in J&H, and Dorrance Sexton was not impressed that the management of Boels & Bégault boasted so many members of the founding families.

Up to now, such servicing in Italy as had been required was carried out by Michael Day flying out from London, which he rather enjoyed. On one such Alitalia flight, Michael found himself sitting next to a particularly attractive young lady. When they reached the Alps, they hit an area of really bad turbulence, and not wishing his attractive companion to feel frightened, Michael lent across and held her hand. The danger over, Michael thought he should at least strike up a conversation with her, and asked her what she did for a living. 'I'm an airline hostess,' came back the reply.

By the time Dorrance Sexton had decided that J&H would set up their European company in Italy, Lloyd Benedict had pretty much decided that he was going to run it. Thus it was that after an early scouting trip in March 1964 to look for premises in Milan, the business capital of Italy, J&H Italy officially opened for business the following month. Lloyd was joined by John Rolland, a young chap from the Montreal office, and they hired as their secretary Caterina Scalise, the daughter of the manager of one of the Italian insurance companies. Rolland quickly decided that Italy was not the place for him, and he certainly wasn't going to bring his future bride to live in Milan. The final straw was when the summer came and Caterina moved into sleeveless dresses: it was painfully obvious that she didn't shave under her arms. Poor John simply couldn't bear to look at her, and told Lloyd that enough was enough. But he agreed to stay on until a replacement could be found.

It is difficult to imagine anyone more international than Rudi Portaria. Born in Shanghai of a Portuguese father and Swedish mother, he was educated in a French school and joined the Swedish merchant marine to get away from China. Ending up

* J&H had previously asked Jauch & Hübener whether they would be prepared to re-open in Italy, but they declined.

in Montreal in 1951 and wanting something different, he tried his hand at college but soon dropped out. Then a chance encounter with the secretary of the London & Lancashire Insurance Company found him joining the insurance industry, and working his way up to be a city inspector. In the meantime he had acquired Canadian citizenship and married his German wife Margrit, whom he met on a blind date. Always on the lookout for a new opportunity, he was persuaded to join J&H Montreal in 1961 by the casualty manager, Sid Ritchie.

In those days the Montreal office was under the guiding hand of Paddy Stephenson and used to hold a very elaborate Christmas party at the city race track, which by then was closed until the next season. This was the insurance social event of the

Rudi Portaria

Brusela/Feb.93

year, attended by clients, underwriters, and city dignitaries. Rudi was cornered by a somewhat unstable Ward Chase, the rather thirsty J&H director responsible for Canada, waving a glass of champagne at him. 'Portaria, Portaria, is that Italian?' 'No sir,' said Rudi, 'Portuguese.' 'That's a pity,' came back the reply, 'because we're thinking of opening an office in Italy.' Rudi quickly assured him that with his background he would have no difficulty learning Italian, and would be very interested. 'Come and see me in the morning,' said Chase, before lurching off in the direction of more champagne.

Rudi was left wondering whether he would ever remember this conversation in the morning, but took the precaution of talking it through with Margrit when he got home. Chase was at his desk bright-eyed and bushy-tailed the next morning, remembered every word of the previous night's conversation, and arranged then and there for Rudi to take Italian lessons at Berlitz. This was in December 1962; 1963 came and went, and it was not till the spring of 1964 that he got a telephone call from someone called Peter Bickett in New York asking what on earth he was doing in Montreal when he should have been in Milan. Such was Rudi Portaria's introduction to J&H international.

After a few months in New York for training, Rudi joined Lloyd in Milan in September 1964, and they both set about visiting the Italian subsidiaries of J&H's clients, while attempting to learn the language. Trying to convince the Italians of anything to do with insurance was pretty difficult, and well-nigh impossible unless you could speak Italian. Lloyd's solution was to lie in the bath reading out loud the daily reports in *Oggi* of the particularly messy divorce of Gina Lollobrigida, an Italian actress whose sexual activities were gripping the nation. Presumably he ended up with a pretty interesting vocabulary. He and Rudi both made progress, congratulating themselves after one meeting that they could now understand each other's Italian, even if the underwriter in question couldn't. But it eventually became clear that they must hire an Italian-speaking member of staff and Carmine Maffei, an employee of Wilcox Baringer, J&H's reinsurance subsidiary, who had been acting until then as unofficial adviser and interpreter, suggested employing his cousin. In the absence of any other alternative, Lloyd agreed.

Italo Maffei arrived on Monday morning. The most noticeable thing about him was his suit, which looked as though it had been bought for him when he was sixteen. Every button of his jacket was done up, just, and he had white socks. He certainly spoke Italian, but he didn't speak anything else. It wasn't a question of interviewing him – he had come to start work, so Lloyd Benedict decided he had better stay. It was the best decision he ever made, because this meek, deferential young Italian was to become one of the mainstays of J&H Italy. He was the most unbelievable worker, and had a dogged persistence that became renowned throughout the Italian insurance market. He started off by memorising the Italian civil code – he must have read it every night before going to bed – and armed with this knowledge would challenge every underwriter. His most deadly broking tactic was to refuse to leave until he had got what he wanted, prompting one underwriter to plead with Lloyd not to send him again. Lloyd Benedict spent much of his time outside Italy, being heavily involved on behalf of Dorrance Sexton in the development and encouragement of the embryonic European network, but he was determined that the fledgling Italian operation would be seen in the best possible light by the board in New York. If it was not exactly in profit, he was at pains to ensure that any loss was kept to a minimum.

The company car, a 1964 Opel, was to be used for company business as well as Lloyd's own personal use. If he was out of town, it had to be garaged in the company parking space. No one really objected to this arrangement – he was the boss after all – but they did object to his habit of never putting gas in the car. Time and again someone would be taking the car on a client visit, and it would run out of gas two blocks from the office in heavy Milan traffic, leaving them to enlist the help of some passer-by to push them into the side of the road, often assisted by a white-helmeted, whistle-blowing *poliziotto*.

In 1966 Benedict returned to New York to become head of international operations reporting to Dick Henshaw, and was replaced by Ken Withers. Withers had his own small broking firm in Texas, but feeling like a change of scenery in more ways than one, had moved to Rio de Janeiro, leaving his wife firmly in Texas. Here he was hired by J&H, and subsequently moved to Venezuela where he eventually took over as country manager when Bill Bumsted returned to New York.

Ken Withers was extremely well versed in all the good things in life, and an excellent host, but knew next to nothing about insurance. He only had one foreign language, a sort of Esperanto which he called French when in France, Spanish when in Spain, Italian when in Italy, but the words were all the same. He also had the disconcerting habit of arriving at meetings without pen or paper. He would borrow a pen, rip open a cigarette packet to make notes on, and then at the end of the meeting either leave the notes behind or toss everything into the waste-paper basket.

He would always boast about his 'yacht' moored at Rapallo, and invite people to make use of it when they were in the area. All they had to do, he said, was to make themselves known to Giovanni the boat keeper, and they would be on their way. A group of five decided to take Ken up on his kind offer and one Saturday morning, hampers in hand, arrived at the dock to seek out Giovanni. They thought that Giovanni reacted rather strangely but followed him down the quay all the same, passing one luxury yacht after another until finally the moment of truth arrived – there moored between two such yachts was a twelve-foot rubber dinghy equipped with an outboard motor!

On another occasion Ken succeeded in parking his car on the streetcar tracks – not any streetcar tracks, but the ones connecting Stazione Centrale to the city centre. The tracks run on a grassy island separating the wide boulevard, and with parking always at a premium in Milan, Ken couldn't understand why the locals didn't make use of this grassy patch. He saw the tracks all right, but because of the overgrown and untrimmed grass, figured they must have been abandoned. He parked, locked his car, and went about his business, leaving behind a chaotic transportation problem for the city.

He did however bring in one insurance innovation – selling

Difference in Conditions (DIC)* policies for one dollar, something that has never been done before or since.

One day Ken returned from a particularly good lunch and fell asleep at his desk. When he awoke, there was the local parish priest standing over him giving him a blessing, complete with an altar boy doing the business with the incense. Poor Ken, he must have thought that his final hour had come and the last rites were being administered. This was the Italian custom of the local priest coming in to bless all homes and offices at New Year in return for a donation.

Some time in 1966 when Ken Withers was off for an extended period with hepatitis, a memo was received in the office addressed to him from Dick Purnell, who was then the director in charge of the Philadelphia office. The risk manager of Rohm & Haas, a very import client of J&H Philadelphia, would be visiting Milan, and Purnell wanted everything to go smoothly. Rudi Portaria as assistant manger of the office immediately replied to Purnell saying everything would be fine and he would handle the visit personally. Several days later a telegram (there were no faxes in those days) was received from Purnell addressed to John Noble who had recently joined the Milan office from New York to say that he had received a reply from Portaria saying that he would handle this very important visit, but did Mr Portaria speak English because the risk manager spoke no Italian? Rudi immediately telexed back to Purnell in Italian: 'Caro Sig. Purnell, Abbiamo ricevuto il tuo messaggio. . .' – 'Dear Mr Purnell, We have received your message of . . . Do not be concerned about my ability to speak English. As I have spoken it since childhood I will be quite capable of conversing with your important client. We know the importance of this account to you, and will send you a full report following the visit.' Several days later another telex came from Purnell, 'Caro Sig. Portaria, Grazie, Grazie. Arrivederci.'

Rudi had completely forgotten about this incident until he was visiting the Philadelphia office some months later, and was told Dick Purnell, whom he had never met, wanted to see him.

* A DIC policy brought the cover provided by an underlying policy up to 'All Risks'.

Werner Zeitler, who then handled the international desk, said it was something to do with a telex Rudi had sent in Italian. He was ushered into the presence, and there was a big, athletic, sun-tanned man, not the sort you wanted to get the wrong side of. Getting up from behind his desk he said, 'Portaria, you wop bastard. Do you know the trouble I had getting your telex translated? I knew, the moment I received it that you didn't speak English!'* Not long afterwards, Purnell was transferred to New York as the next president of J&H.

One day Rudi received out of the blue a large demand for *Imposta di Famiglia*, the family tax that was supposedly based on the size of your house and standard of living. The locals knew the trick of not letting the inspectors come in and measure the rooms in the first place or, if they did come in, plying them with hospitality, but not the luckless foreigners. Fortunately, the risk manager of Ferrania had told Rudi if he ever had any problems with the tax people to just let him know, as he had very good relations with the *Guardia di Finanza*, the financial police. A call was duly made, and Rudi was told there would be no problems – they would get in touch with him.

Some time later in the office, a scared Claudia Giacomelli came to tell Rudi that a uniformed member of the *Guardia di Finanza* was there to see him. Rudi thought that he ought to have a witness, so on the pretence that his Italian wasn't terribly good, he asked Claudia to attend the meeting. Once the problem had been explained to him, the helpful policeman asked to see the tax demand and, sucking his teeth, asked Rudi how much he would like to pay. Rudi came up with a figure of some twenty-five per cent of the initial demand, and the policeman said he thought that that would be possible. 'But', he said, 'we have a scale', and Rudi had to pay a certain percentage of the reduction. There was a slight problem with Sherwood Bonney, the chief financial officer of J&H in New York, when Rudi put 'bribe' down on his expenses claim, but it was eventually sorted out.

In 1968 Withers was replaced as manager of J&H Italy by Charlie Anthony. Ken Withers transferred to Willis in London at

* As recounted by Rudi Portaria.

the request of Ronnie Taylor, a request that Ronnie would soon live to regret. Ken arrived with Leno, his 'man for all things', to become J&H's resident representative in London. It soon became apparent that although he was excellent at looking after visiting J&H clients, he did not know the insurance business, and his sexual orientation was giving cause for concern. To top it all, he found himself working closely with Michael Day, who simply had no time for someone who promised what he couldn't deliver. 'With-ahs, where's With-ahs?' would be heard ringing down the third-floor corridor of 54 Leadenhall Street. The stories are legion, and the majority are better left untold. By the time Ken Withers left London at the end of 1974, Ronnie Taylor vowed they would never ever have a resident representative from J&H again. After a short time in New York, he was sent to Brockman y Schuh in Mexico, where he finally came out of the closet, and had to leave J&H.

Charlie Anthony joined the property department in New York from the Factory Mutuals, and was responsible for building the strong team of insurance professionals that were to make J&H the leading broker in Italy. Ken Seward, who took over in 1973, really inspired and put to work the team that Anthony had put together.

In 1972, J&H Italy opened their second office, in Rome, to be run by co-managers Italo Maffei and Paolo Carega. They couldn't have been more different. Italo was the epitome of the self-made man who had got to where he was through sheer determination and hard work; Paolo was the Harvard-educated son of an Italian diplomat who had originally joined J&H as a trainee in Boston in 1969 before being transferred to New York. He was tall, impeccably dressed, married to a rich American wife, and drove a Ferrari. Italo was small, dumpy, and definitely used a different tailor. All the concierge wanted to know when they opened the Rome office was which was Mr Johnson and which Mr Higgins?

No one exemplified the unusual and talented cast of characters in the Milan office more than Gianni Zunino. With his RAF handle-bar moustache, upper-crust English accent and smart braces (suspenders), he might be mistaken for the product of an

Oxford or Cambridge college. In fact he had been born in the picturesque village of Ormea south-west of Milan, where his father was a stonemason. He always wanted to learn languages, so after a course in modern languages he moved to Germany where a friend gave him a job in his travel agency. After eighteen months he moved to England, which had always been his ultimate goal. Here he enrolled in the Holborn College of Law and Languages in London, and to help support himself, worked as a waiter in the Captain's Room* at Lloyd's. He quickly became a favourite among the regulars, Ken Childs (who was then still at Minet), Derek Martin of Willis (who also had an RAF handle-bar moustache) and Frank Barber, who went on to become a deputy chairman of Lloyd's. Frank took a great interest in Gianni, and one day asked him if he wouldn't like to do something better than just wait on tables. 'Well, I will eventually, but right now . . .' 'Why don't you come and see me?' Frank replied, and Gianni was in his office that very afternoon. In no time at all, he had been introduced to David Palmer and Alan Parry of Sedgwick, and received job offers from both. He was in two minds which to accept, but Sedgwick was offering more money. 'Go with Willis for less,' said Barber, 'it's a much better path for you.' So he went to work in the Willis overseas department with Michael Day in 1964, and eventually for Ken Childs after he had joined Willis.

Gianni never intended to leave the UK; he had an English wife and two children, was a very keen tennis player, and also played classical guitar with a group of other musicians. But one day in 1971 he had a call from Charlie Anthony inviting him to go for an interview with J&H in Milan, all expenses paid. Charlie was very persuasive, and Gianni agreed to go to Milan for two or three years. He ended up staying for ten, and only left after he was persuaded by Ken Seward to transfer to Hartford, Connecticut, to take over responsibility for the very demanding United Technologies account.

Ken Seward really drove the business forward. All the talent was there – Franco Fratini, Paolo Rizzo, Lionel de Costa, David Sweetman, Carlo Locatelli, Adriano Gazzaniga, Simone Sacco –

* The members' restaurant.

CHIP TALKING ON RISK MANAGEMENT!

he just put it to work. The third office opened in Padua in 1978, followed by Bologna in 1982 and Torino in 1987. For the first ten years almost all the business came from US multinationals, but by 1979 more than fifty per cent was indigenous business. J&H had penetrated the Italian market.

When the time came for Seward's tour of duty to come to an end in 1979, he knew that there was only one person who could take over from him – Bob Beane. Fortunately, although still in Gil y Carvajal, Beane was by then on the J&H payroll, so what seemed to Seward at the time a difficult move was completed with comparative ease. Bob Beane in his turn was to hand over to Chip Bechtold in 1984. Chip had started with the Factory Mutuals and joined J&H in 1976. His interview with Lloyd Benedict became a mere formality after the first five minutes when Lloyd discovered that they had both been in the same fraternity house, Phi Delta Theta. He rose to become manager of the international department in New York before taking over in Italy.

It was not until Chip moved back to New York in 1990 that the first Italian took over as manager, Franco Fratini. He was supported by Jim Hutchin, who acted as branch manager in Milan and represented Italy on the PWG.* Franco's promotion caused quite an upheaval in J&H Italy and Italo Maffei, among others, left. But as is so often the case in such situations, the correct decision had been made, and Franco in his turn drove the Italian company forward. An interesting, cultured man, he had joined the *Carabinieri* in 1959, rising to the rank of *Vice Brigadiere* by the time he left in 1962. Quiet-mannered but determined, Franco went through a total change at weekends when he donned his leathers and helmet and went roaring along the roads around his home town of Pisa on his Harley Davidson. There is always more to the Italians than meets the eye.

* See chapter 11.

9 The Belgians, the Dutch, the Danes, the Swiss, and the Greeks

It must be fairly depressing living somewhere that has been invaded by neighbours quite so many times, but the Belgians are basically a happy people living in an unremarkable little country. But it does have one tremendous thing going for it – the food. Even the fries are to die for, and as for the desserts . . . If any serious gastronome was offered one last dinner anywhere in the world, that dinner would have to be in Belgium.

But beneath a placid exterior the country is riven by deep division, the most obvious outward sign of which is the language. Visit the French-speaking part round the town of Courtrai, and it's difficult to believe that you're not still in France. But the Flemish-speaking area around Antwerp is like a different country. This is so fundamental that every company in a service industry has both French- and Flemish-speaking staff. Brussels is considered neutral territory, so all official communications including street signs must be in Flemish and French. One golf club solved the problem by having everything in English.

Through no fault of the Belgians, Brussels was to become the international centre for a totally new twentieth-century industry – bureaucracy. With the headquarters of the European Community in Brussels, not to mention the North Atlantic Treaty Organisation, better known as NATO, there was a boom in all manner of administrative support industries, from secretaries to real estate agencies, but above all interpreters. Suddenly, a country that was in danger of becoming relegated to the second division found itself at the very centre of Europe. The potential was all too apparent to the grand old man of the Belgian insurance market, Emile Bégault.

Boels & Bégault was founded by Fritz Boels in 1908, but was not incorporated until he went into partnership with his brother-in-law, Emile Bégault, in 1920. Emile Bégault was to totally dominate the firm, and build it to be the leading insurance broker in Belgium. He was a hard-working man, not unlike

General Franco in appearance, but in temperament more like General de Gaulle. He brought into the firm a number of his relations, and one of his sons-in-law, Léon Delacroix, and a nephew, Lucien Bégault, both became partners. Trying to sort out the structure of the firm with all its interrelated small companies, which even included a BMW and a Honda agency at one time, was almost as bad as trying to find your way back through the rabbit warren that existed inside the collection of old houses in the rue des Chevaliers which served as the firm's head office.

Meanwhile, Daniel Kervyn de Meerendré had married one of Emile Bégault's daughters, and the old man didn't think that working for Sabena, the national airline, was going to keep her in the manner to which she was accustomed. Dany therefore joined Boels & Bégault in 1955, and worked with Henri Marcette who was responsible for Boels & Bégault's operations in the Belgian Congo. Dany was the son of a Belgian diplomat. His mother died when he was only eighteen months old, and he learned his excellent English from an English nanny while living in Canada.

As Uncle Emile, as he became to be known in Willis, didn't speak much English, Dany was called in to translate when Bill Bumsted and Paddy Stephenson arrived on their famous trip. Emile immediately took a great liking to Paddy Stephenson, who was very cultured and spoke perfect French. Bumsted on the other hand was every European's idea of an American – a huge man with a cigar permanently clenched between his teeth, which made him even more difficult to understand. Emile thought at any moment he might put his feet on his desk. But Emile quickly saw that a relationship with J&H would greatly assist him in getting the better of his main competitor, Henrijean, so he was only too pleased to accept their proposals. This had to be followed up by a presentation to the J&H directors in New York before it could be ratified.

Emile and Dany went over to New York. Emile also wanted J&H to accept his office in Paris as their French correspondent, and woke Dany up at 5.00 a.m. to get him to draft a contract to that effect. But J&H had no intention of doing this, and Emile, who was used to always getting his own way, grew increasingly nervous as the meeting progressed. Finally he stood up, gathered his files together, dropped them on the floor with a crash, and with his hands still hanging down between his legs said in his broken English, 'Je suis fed up with hearing these men talking of my Balls and Bégault.' With that he marched out of the room, slamming the door behind him, leaving a petrified Dany surrounded by a dozen J&H directors. To his immense relief, they all burst out laughing, and someone said, 'He, at least, has what he said.' So agreement was reached, but for Belgium only.

Once when Michael Day and David Palmer were visiting Boels & Bégault, Uncle Emile was trying to impress on one of his young staff the importance of learning English. 'See,' he said, 'Mr Day speaks French and Mr Palmer tries to speak French.' Both were probably a slight exaggeration.

On the death of Emile Bégault, Lucien stepped into his shoes, and Dany became the partner responsible for the future UNISON business. Lucien was extremely well respected in the Belgium market, and a great friend of Willis Faber's. He formed a highly successful joint reinsurance company with Willis, and the Boels & Bégault subsidiary in Lisbon went on to become the UNISON partner for Portugal. In some ways he was quite a formal man. One night he had been working late, and as he let himself out of the front door of the office he was immediately propositioned by one of the ladies of the night who used to make a habit at that time of using the entrance to 13 rue des Chevaliers as her beat. '*Non merci*,' he said politely, 'I have everything I need at home.'

In addition to their neighbours, the Dutch have had to contend periodically with being invaded by the sea. They have always been a seafaring nation, earnest, hard-working and rather humourless when compared with the peoples of southern Europe. According to tradition, it is possible to buy shirts in Rotterdam with the sleeves already rolled up. But as always, a few make up for the many, both in humour and in alcohol consumption.

The origins of Mees & zoonen go back to 1 January 1720 when Gregorius Mees became a partner in the firm of Cordelois

De Vrijer (founded in 1684), more than one hundred and forty years before the formation of either Willis Faber or J&H. The activities of this firm were simple deposit banking, bill broking and insurance broking. In 1733, both senior partners of the firm retired and Gregorius Mees took over. Later he was joined by his three sons and the name of the firm changed to R. Mees & zoonen in 1786. His family motto, *Wakker zijn en het midden houden* ('Be vigilant and steer a middle course'), was to guide the Mees family as they built a banking and insurance empire that was headed exclusively by family members for one hundred and sixty-nine years.

Mees & zoonen, being then predominantly marine brokers, prospered with the expansion of the port of Rotterdam, strategically placed at the mouth of the river Maas. This was virtually destroyed during World War II, but by 1952 post-war construction had continued at such a pace that Rotterdam's commerce surpassed its best pre-war years. In 1962, the firm joined forces with Hope & Co., another illustrious Dutch financial dynasty. At the end of the year, the insurance activities were transferred to an independent company which retained the Mees & zoonen name. This became part of Algemene Bank Nederland (ABN) in 1975.

The relationship between Mees & zoonen and J&H goes back to the 1920s, when Rudolf Mees offered J&H a share of the Holland America Line and Royal Rotterdam Lloyd fleet insurances. The relationship was broken during the war, but was picked up soon afterwards when Peter Mees and Kir Verbeek re-established the placing relationship with the J&H marine department. On a subsequent visit to Rotterdam, a J&H marine director thanked Mr Mees for all his time and a splendid lunch, but said he would also like to meet Mr Zoonen – little realising that this was Dutch for 'sons'.

The two people in Mees & zoonen best-known in the UNISON network were Aad Strijbos and Gert van de Sande. Strijbos was the brilliant and extremely hard-working manager of the property department who went on to become chairman and managing director. Very much a man of the people, he was as likely to be found having a beer with the serving staff after

Gert van de Sande

excusing himself from the top table at some formal banquet as mingling with the important guests. A larger-than-life character who always led from the front, he became the international face of Mees & zoonen. Gert van de Sande originally joined the marine underwriting subsidiary in 1970, but transferred to Mees & zoonen in 1975. He became commercial director responsible for all the account managers and joined the PWG (see Chapter 11) in 1982. A kind, likeable fellow with good English, he was always hampered by the time it took him to translate the conversation into Dutch. It was all too easy for the Brits and Americans to forget that English wasn't everyone's first language.

It was Strijbos who introduced the first Mees & zoonen client to the J&H international network in 1967 with the help of his great Willis Faber friend, David Slade. Mees & zoonen were to go on to produce many major global clients for UNISON.

The history and temperament of the Danes closely follows that of the British, with whom they have long stood shoulder to shoulder. An open, quarrelsome people, always asking questions, they eventually joined the European Union on the same day as the UK.

To UNISON, Denmark meant John Bonnor. He was a hard-working, likeable, pipe-smoking chap who always looked as though he had just got out of bed in rather a hurry, and the Liverpool, London & Globe Insurance Company didn't know what to make of their Danish trainee when he arrived in Liverpool on secondment from the Baltica in 1960. He was persuaded to exchange his black shirt, grey tie and leather jacket for a suit, but not before he had sold his motorbike to pay for it. He was so hard up when he transferred to the local payroll that he could no longer afford the bus fare, so came in by bicycle, much to the chagrin of his employers, who insisted he use the tradesmen's entrance. In 1962 he was seconded to Wellington, New Zealand, by which time he was engaged to a lady in the claims department. He left without her, and worked evenings in a fish and chip shop so they could scrape together the money for Anne to come out and get married.

Returning to Denmark in 1965, he eventually was approached by Marsh & McLennan to start a brokerage company, Dahl Jørgensen, in 1977, but this didn't prosper, and Bonnor was left with an extreme distrust of all things American. It was a Brit, John Shaw of Hinton Hill in London, who persuaded him to set up Bonnor & Co. in 1979 to handle their Danish portfolio. By the following year things had gone so well that John had gained financial control of the company. It was then appointed to place the business for a major power station jointly with a firm of German brokers, which turned out to be Jauch & Hübener. Oschi Hübener was so impressed with the Bonnor presentation that he arranged to come over and meet John, and Anne (the only other employee) brought two more chairs from home so that Oschi would have somewhere to sit. They hit it off immediately, and from then on Oschi Hübener was an important influence on John Bonnor, eventually joining the board of the company in 1981 after he had retired. Oschi put Bonnor in touch with Willis to help with some aviation business, which went very well, and shortly afterwards Bonnor severed his link with Hinton Hill.

By this time word had reached J&H that John Bonnor had formed the first credible brokerage in Denmark but, ever mistrustful of Americans, he would have nothing to do with them. It was only when Oschi persuaded John that he had made a great mistake, and he had been introduced to Peter Bickett, that the link with the future UNISON was formed, in 1982. John Bonnor was to go on to be the only UNISON partner to sell a share of his company to UNISON SA.

Although they play a relatively minor part in the overall story, no review of the future UNISON partners would be complete without mentioning the Swiss and the Greeks. Switzerland is a country unlike any other. A mountainous enclave that skilfully managed to maintain its neutrality through both world wars, it is a country where the streets are clean and the trains run on time. Every able-bodied man above the age of nineteen has to do military training as a member of the large bicycling army, then a two-week refresher course every year for ten years. Once it's completed, the men go home and put their rifles back in their bedroom cupboards. Not surprisingly, the Swiss are serious, hard-working and extremely organised. They have long been the legendary financiers of Europe. All the world loves the Swiss franc, but only the Swiss love the centime.

Kessler & Co. was started in 1918 by Johann Kessler as a general agent specialising in marine and transport insurance. Under the guidance of his son Hans Kessler, who took over the firm in 1956, it went through major expansion to become the largest broker in Switzerland, handling all lines of insurance.

The relationship with J&H began in 1969, when J&H Italy, who had previously been responsible for servicing in Switzerland, entered negotiations which resulted in a correspondent agreement the following year. But Hans Kessler was a wily old bird, and had no intention of entering an exclusive agreement with anyone. It was only after his eldest son Martin, who was to go on to become chief executive, had spent two very successful years working in J&H New York from 1980 that he agreed to join the UNISON network. Martin had realised that to be successful, Kessler needed access to an international network.

In addition to being extremely good insurance men, Martin and his younger brother Robert are phenomenal golfers and skiers. They have both been members of the Swiss national golf team, and Martin went on to be captain.

Greece is a country of great antiquity, but for many it is the place where they had an unforgettable holiday in their youth and an energetic night with a waiter or waitress (or both) after too much sun and wine. It is another country of great contrasts: the beauty and solitude of some of the more remote islands, and in Athens some of the worst traffic jams in the world.

As with Switzerland, servicing J&H clients in Greece was originally carried out by J&H Italy, but after a time it became necessary to find someone to provide service locally. Rudi Portaria happened to be visiting Peter Fornacca, manager of AFIA Italy, and knowing they had operations in Greece, asked him if there was anyone he could recommend. No problem, said Fornacca, because there was only one 'honest' broker in Greece, Demitri (Taky) Tarpohzy of Mercury Insurance Agencies. The fact that Taky was also the authorised agent for AFIA would not create any conflict, because he was an 'honest Greek'.

A week or two later, Rudi was in Athens, so went to meet Taky at his office. The offices had been freshly painted and the smell hung in the air; Rudi couldn't help wondering whether they had been painted for his benefit. Taky turned out to be an older man, but he was alert, spoke a multitude of languages, knew the insurance business inside out, and what was expected of a broker. He was also a connoisseur of food and wine, and the discussion continued over dinner at a chic restaurant. Rudi was very impressed, but then, as the two of them were talking at the table, Taky's eyes closed and he appeared to be asleep. Somewhat disconcerted, Rudi wondered whether he should gently nudge him, when all of a sudden his eyes opened and he continued the conversation where he had left off. Taky had a medical condition which meant he would drop off to sleep without any warning.

Rudi reported back to New York that Taky had a number of very positive points, but was a bit concerned that he might be too old. Thirty years later, when most of those involved at the time had long since retired, Taky was still working. Even Taky

Serbos, who had been hired in anticipation of his retirement, retired before Taky Tarpohzy.

Christian Dahms was sitting next to Taky in an afternoon meeting when, true to form, Taky closed his eyes and went to sleep. Christian lit up one of his little cigars and, not finding an ashtray close to hand, used his coffee cup. Shortly afterwards Taky woke up, and drank the remains of the coffee, apparently oblivious of the additives.

In the autumn of 1985, J&H invited all the European members of UNISON to New York to attend a series of presentations focusing on the hardening US casualty market. By far the most senior presenter was Hank Greenberg, legendary chief executive and driving force behind the American Insurance Group (AIG), the most important US casualty insurer. Five minutes into the presentation, the door opened, and in walked Taky. He looked around the packed room and saw an empty seat, immediately in front of the presenter. 'I don't believe it,' said Seward under his breath, 'he's going to take that seat.' Not being used to this sort of treatment, Greenberg stopped and his eyes followed Taky as he sat down directly in front of him. Then Greenberg resumed his presentation, and Taky closed his eyes and went to sleep.

Taky Tarpohzy

10 The Annual Conference

Now that the founding members of UNISON have all been described, it's time to return to our story. Once the major building blocks of the European network were in place, business started to be introduced to the new correspondent brokers, but there was not much sign of cohesion or uniformity. Lloyd Benedict believed that it was essential to call all the new correspondents together, and was able to sell this to the New York directors. Emile Bégault offered to act as host, and the first J&H Correspondents' Conference was held in Brussels in February 1965. This was a relatively low-key affair, chaired by Lloyd, but it had the effect of getting representatives from all the European correspondents together to at least meet each other. The second day was spent in introducing the European brokers to J&H's latest international client, ITT, so the very effective idea of presenting all the local servicing brokers to an international client was an early one.

Such was the success of this conference that it was unanimously agreed to repeat the performance, but this time, each correspondent would also send a relatively senior man. The J&H delegation was to be led by the executive vice-president of the firm, Dick Henshaw, who was an impressive man. He served with distinction as a much decorated artillery colonel in World War II. After joining J&H in 1946, he continued in the army reserves, attaining the rank of brigadier-general, so was thenceforth always known as 'The General'. With the new office in Italy only opened the year before, Milan was the obvious choice for the second conference, and J&H set about organising it. Unfortunately Lloyd Benedict selected a somewhat more modest hotel in the business district than most of the partners of the European brokers were used to. It also boasted a number of young ladies who were not apparently staying in the hotel but were just there in case they might be needed. The hospitality suite was in Ken Withers' apartment, and at one point they ran out of Scotch – a problem solved by Dick Henshaw and David Palmer going out over the roof to reach the apartment of someone's girl friend to obtain reinforcements.

An excellent evening was had in one of those typical family-style Italian restaurants. When it was time for the bill, the waiter came and sat down at the table next to David Palmer, wrote out a long calculation and then put the final amount in the top right-hand corner, tore it off, and handed it to David. Without halting the conversation, David Palmer took from his wallet one of the old lira notes which in those days were pretty large, studied it intently for a moment, then tore off the right-hand corner and handed it to the waiter. The expression on the waiter's face had to be seen to be believed.

The other thing that Benedict had not taken into account was the weather. Flying in and out of Milan at any time can be tricky, but in February it is virtually impossible. David Palmer and Michael Day left the final cocktail party early, checked in at the downtown terminal, and caught the airport bus. Somewhere along the route the driver got word that the airport had closed due to fog, and in typical Italian style, the passengers were tipped out then and there and left to their own devices. In no time at all David and Michael were back at the cocktail party, their boarding cards still proudly displayed in their breast pockets. Perhaps the various logistical problems made everyone feel much closer in the face of adversity, but from then on it was unanimously agreed to hold what became an annual conference in May.

It was decided that the conference should rotate round the various countries to give every correspondent the opportunity of hosting, and a rota was drawn up to allow plans to be made ahead. When their turn came round in 1970 Willis took the view that this should be a pretty utilitarian affair, and it was a long time before they lived down the choice of the Esso Motor Hotel outside Maidenhead. Actually this proved a very practical venue, particularly as it was right next to a most excellent restaurant. This gave Willis a great opportunity to sell their wholesaling wares to all the European correspondents, a ploy adroitly repeated every year, much to the irritation of J&H.

As was so often to be the case, all that had gone before paled into insignificance compared with the first conference hosted by Gil y Carvajal in Marbella in 1971. What ever else the Spanish knew, they certainly knew how to entertain and make their guests feel welcome. This had its effect on the entire conference, and for the first time there was a deeper feeling of friendship and understanding, encouraged by the sun and plenty of *Rioja*. The conference ended on the Thursday night with a dinner in a lovely restaurant about six or seven miles from the hotel and the entire company danced and sang till the early hours. About 3 a.m. the party finally left the restaurant, to be ferried back in a fleet of cars driven by their Gil y Carvajal hosts. Joe Dell, who was representing the New York office with his mentor Peter Bickett, got into the back of one of the cars to find Dick Purnell already in the back seat, and Bickett sitting up front next to the driver. Suddenly there was a thump on the rear of the car, and there was Dorrance Sexton sitting on the boot, looking in through the rear window. As there was plenty of room inside, Purnell sent Joe out to bring Sexton in. Sexton sent him back again, accompanied by several words unfit to print. Purnell sent Joe back again, saying, 'Help him down off the trunk [boot].' By this time quite a crowd had gathered to see the chairman of J&H on the boot of the car. 'Don't you dare touch me,' said Sexton. At Purnell's insistence, Joe tried once more, but Sexton declared loudly, 'I'm returning to the hotel in this seat.' Very gingerly, the car set off at about ten miles per hour, with the next car in the convoy keeping a discreet ten lengths behind. As the car pulled up in front of the hotel, Rudi Portaria ran into the moat surrounding the front entrance and got absolutely soaked up to his waist. He claimed in the morning that he had forgotten it was there.

That same conference marked the launch of Euroben, a sort of employee benefits equivalent of UNISON, whose principal progenitors were John McEown, the director responsible for employee benefits in J&H, and Ronnie Taylor of Willis. Euroben was always somewhat of a poor relation, largely because employee benefit business did not respond to international treatment in the same way as the general insurances. To mark the launch, Euroben invited all the delegates to a pre-dinner cocktail party on the second evening. David Palmer was strolling in the hotel grounds with Dorrance Sexton, and asked him if he was planning to attend. 'Sure,' he replied. 'Two dry Martinis is likely to be the only dividend I'll get from that outfit.' How right he was.

One problem that arose was the thorny question of wives. It had begun to be the custom that the partners, as the senior representatives of the various correspondent brokers were called, would take their wives. This was good because the wives quickly made friends with each other, which helped to bind people even more closely together. Then one year there was a bit of a problem: the wives didn't like the hotel, or the food, or the itinerary. Sexton, encouraged by Benedict who thought that they merely increased the cost of the event, decreed that wives would no longer attend. The following year a handful of wives led by Maggie Purnell, Denyse Bégault and Millie Palmer managed to circumvent the ban by staying in a different hotel. It was quite a few years before, bowing to pressure from Oschi and Harald Hübener, wives were once more officially allowed to attend.

The first evening of the conference was always left open, so that delegates could arrange their own groups for dinner. On one such evening a group arranged to go to a particularly out-of-the-way little restaurant, only to find Oschi and Harald Hübener entertaining a couple of ladies to a candle-lit dinner.

As the years went by, the annual conference became a major event, with each country trying to out-do the others in the splendour of the hospitality. There were more and more attendees, and invitations to the fringe groups became highly prized. It also enabled some of the more domestically orientated people in the various correspondent brokers to get a taste of international life, whether they came in the capacity of presenters, account executives, or just lucky invitees.

In 1977 Peter Bickett, who was then manager of the New York international department, suffered a serious injury to his back which kept him away from the office for many months. To help out, George Kadri was brought in from the Detroit office in the capacity of acting international manager. This gave Kadri the opportunity to attend the annual conference and go to Europe, something he hadn't done since the end of the war. On arriving in the bar on the first evenning – the traditional meeting place on such occasions – he mentioned how thoughtful it was of Gras Savoye to have organised a fully stocked bar in his room, but it was such a pity because he only drank beer. 'Don't worry about that, George,' piped up someone already at the bar, 'I'll trade you my beer for your champagne.' George hadn't realised that he would eventually be billed for what had gone from his mini bar, and soon arranged trades for all his liquor and wine, to be repeated on a daily basis. To give him his due, he paid his bill meekly, and never said a word. With memories of Europe at the end of the war, he had also arrived with a supply of toilet paper, in case there wasn't any in his room, and kindly passed this on to someone staying on when he left.

It became customary to provide all delegates with a little present in their hotel rooms at the beginning of the conference, and the Dutch in characteristic style provided a bottle of highly potent Bols Geneva at the Amsterdam conference of 1975. After it was over, Dany Kervyn and Rudi Portaria drove Karl DeFoe (J&H Cleveland) back to Brussels for his next set of meetings. Now, although Karl was quite an experienced international account executive, he was one of those Americans that you would have thought had never ventured out of Ohio. 'We're getting close to the border,' Rudi announced. 'What about the bottle of Geneva?' said Karl. 'Haven't you opened it yet?' said Rudi. 'You've got to have a drink out of it.' They heard the sound of the bottle being opened, and Karl taking a tentative sip. 'You've got to drink more than that,' said Dany, who was driving. Karl took a swig. 'Haven't you opened yours yet, Rudi?' 'No,' said Rudi, 'I don't like it, which is why I left mine in my hotel room. Now take a proper slug, Karl, because we're almost at the border.' Poor Karl took a really large swig, almost choking as he did so, just as they roared into Belgium. Not only was he really mad, but he felt decidedly groggy when he arrived at the office. Ironically, when Karl first arrived in Amsterdam he had asked whether it was safe to drink the water.

As the conferences got bigger and spilt over into a third day, it became the practice to have a free afternoon before the annual dinner. Being the insurance world, this invariably meant golf, a fairly pointless occupation in the eyes of some – you can't even eat the thing at the end of the day. Once the partners, who naturally had the first tee-off times, were assembling in the lobby of the hotel beforehand. Harald Hübener came down first with a most impressive set of Ping golf clubs, followed by Paddy Satrústegui with the most beautiful Spanish leather golf bag, then Lucien Bégault with the latest Louis Vuitton golf bag bristling with clubs, and finally Michael Day, with four old clubs wrapped in newspaper. Michael won.

By the beginning of the 1980s the annual UNISON conference, as it had become, really was UNISON as far as some of the partners were concerned. Perhaps mindful of the Esso Motor Hotel thirteen years before, Willis (or at least Michael Day) organised the 1983 conference at Claridges, one of the best hotels in London. All went well until the day of departure when the first people went to pay their bill – Claridges didn't take American Express.

The following year, Gras Savoye were the hosts at St Paul de Vence in the south of France, a marvellous spot up in the hills above Nice. On the first evening, after an extremely good dinner, a group were loitering by the swimming pool when Rudi Portaria, ever hopeful, bent down to kiss a frog that was minding its own business in the corner of the pool. Another frog that happened to be passing gave him a gentle nudge, and Rudi ended up in the pool in his best light-weight suit complete with passport, French francs, and his presentation for the following morning. Rudi having shown the way, everyone decided to have an after-dinner swim, followed by an impromptu party in Mike Barrett's room. This was greatly helped by most bringing not only the contents of their mini-bars, but the actual mini-bars themselves.

David Palmer had joined the conference late because of a particularly hectic schedule, and his eyes closed after lunch on the first day. This was immortalised by Javier Barcaiztegui in a drawing, 'The Chairman's Siesta'.

In 1985 it was the turn of the Spanish again, who arranged to hold the conference in the beautiful Punta Romana hotel in Marbella. This offered the unexpected added attraction of topless bathing – a totally new phenomenon for most of the delegates. Harald Hübener, Michael Day and Jeremy Cohen (who ran employee benefits for Willis) had arrived early, and readily fell into conversation with three ladies of a certain age who were topping up their tan beside the pool. As the first evening was always left free for ad hoc dinners, it seemed an excellent idea to invite these three ladies – an invitation that was readily accepted. Harald, Michael and Jeremy duly arrived down in the lobby at the allotted hour, and the three ladies swept in, dressed to the nines. Just at that very moment, Bob Hatcher, who was by then chairman of J&H, and his wife Martha Anne also appeared in the lobby, looking for dinner guests. Harald Hübener quickly decided that it might be much wiser to have dinner with the Hatchers, and Jeremy Cohen suddenly remembered a very important phone call he hadn't made, so Michael Day was left to get rid of the ladies. Inevitably they bumped into them again during the evening, dining alone, and had to pretend that they had never met them.

Whilst always tremendous fun and very rewarding for the delegates, these conferences became somewhat of a nightmare to organise. To find a hotel of sufficient quality that could accommodate the required number of people, had conference facilities, and was accessible, not to mention having interesting places to visit and high-quality restaurants in the vicinity, was itself quite a problem, and bookings had to be made more than a year in advance. Sometimes the dates themselves caused a problem, but never more so than when Mees & zoonen held the 1990 conference in Rotterdam on the fiftieth anniversary of the German bombing of the city. And however careful the planning, things could still go wrong. The Hatchers retired to bed in the presidential suite after the successful opening dinner of the Rome conference in 1987, only to find that they were immediately underneath the discothèque – which presumably gave an entirely new meaning to the label 'Eternal City'. The conference never recovered.

1989 saw a departure from the normal sequence when the

conference was held in Sweden to coincide with the centenary celebrations of the founding of AB Max Matthiessen, which had joined the network in 1984. Insurance brokers had never been a feature of the Swedish market, which was dominated by several major insurance companies, but Max Matthiessen was the shining exception. Very much the family firm run in a management style more reminiscent of the nineteenth than the twentieth century, it was led by a quiet unassuming man, Göran Groth. But put him behind a piano and all his inhibitions disappeared, as he was immediately transformed into an extremely good one-man music hall act. The climax of the midsummer conference was an open-air party in the grounds of the Groth family mansion, an event that put Max Matthiessen firmly on the UNISON map.

In 1991, Kessler & Co. hosted the conference in Zurich to coincide with the seven-hundredth anniversary of the founding of the State of Switzerland, and in 1995 J&H were hosts in Washington, DC to mark the hundred-and-fiftieth anniversary of J&H. This was the only time the conference was held outside Europe.

Over time, the annual conference became the focal point of the UNISON year. It was an opportunity to renew old friendships, make new ones, do some serious work, and have fun in the best surroundings that the host country could provide. Perhaps too, it epitomised the UNISON network more accurately than any of us realised at the time.

Göran Groth

B.

11 The PWG

As more and more delegates attended the annual conferences in the early 1970s, and the cast tended to change from one year to the next, it became increasingly difficult to concentrate on the standardisation of operating procedures, which had become the major issue with the rapid growth of new business. What was needed, thought Christian Dahms, was someone at the operating level to represent each network partner; these representatives would all work together on operating issues on an ongoing basis. At the 1975 Amsterdam conference Christian ran his ideas past Peter Bickett, who had been thinking along very similar lines. As Bickett, in his capacity as manager of the New York international department, was helping Dick Purnell to run the meetings the following day, it was an easy matter to get this on the agenda.

The idea was to have a permanent group of operational people who would work on the issues of the day, and give recommendations to the partners to ratify. The partners thought this was an excellent idea, because in the majority of cases they had long since ceased to handle accounts on a day-to-day basis, and were finding it difficult to fill the conference agenda. At this stage there was an exchange of notes between Bickett and Purnell:

BICKETT: What are we going to call this group?

PURNELL: It's going to consist of permanent members, and they're going to be working on operational issues, so how about 'Permanent Working Group'?

BICKETT: I don't think that's a very good idea.

PURNELL: You forget whose idea it is.

BICKETT: I think it's a very good idea.

David Palmer also thought that it wasn't a very good idea, pointing out that everyone was working, but as no one could come up with anything better, Purnell's suggestion was accepted. And so the Permanent Working Group, better known as the PWG, came into being. It was then a question of choosing the members. As J&H naturally wanted to control things, Peter

Bickett was proposed as chairman with Rudi Portaria as secretary. Rudi had moved from Milan to Brussels in 1973 and was now responsible for co-ordination of J&H's European clients, based with Boels & Bégault. The other original members were Christian Dahms for Jauch & Hübener, Dany Kervyn for Boels & Bégault, Wim van der Have for Mees & zoonen, Ken Seward for J&H Italy, Bob Beane for Gil y Carvajal, Hugh Hausman and Henri Sommer for Gras Savoye and Ronnie Westhorp for Willis. George Rainoff also appeared at some stage when he was based in Athens with a particularly Rainoff-style roving commission.

Ronnie Westhorp was a very interesting man with a wonderfully dry sense of humour. He joined C.T.Bowring in 1937, but

Ronnie Westhorp

left to join the RAF in 1942. He was sent to flying school in Vancouver, where he had the singular distinction of being the only member of the RAF to successfully ditch a Hampden bomber in the sea, thereby earning membership of the prestigious RAF Goldfish Club. After training at Paignton in Devon, Flight Lieutenant Westhorp flew Lancaster bombers on Pathfinder missions over Germany. At the end of the war, he flew over Holland dropping food to the Dutch. On being discharged from the RAF in 1945, he joined London brokers Griffiths Tait and specialised in film business, eventually joining Willis in 1960. Excellent company, and very entertaining whenever there was a piano in easy reach, he headed up Willis's dedicated team dealing with incoming business from J&H from the time it was set up in 1973. During an early annual conference in Germany, a party of delegates was being taken by bus along the Rhine and the guide pointed out an extremely impressive old bridge. 'I think we must have missed that one,' said Ronnie, in a loud stage whisper overheard by the entire bus.

The PWG immediately got to work and the first meeting was scheduled for October in Hamburg, so that everyone could attend some meeting of risk managers in Copenhagen afterwards. With his usual precision, Peter Bickett had drawn up a lengthy agenda and kept everyone hard at work the entire day. He must have been at least a third of the way through his list when the door was flung open about 6 p.m. and Harald Hübener wheeled in a huge trolley of drinks. 'Oh shit,' said Bickett, throwing down his pencil, realising that he had lost his audience. The principal job of Rudi as secretary was to produce the minutes of the meetings, but everyone knew that these were written by Bickett. Peter was a great believer in that old adage that 'he who writes the minutes dictates what was said at the meeting', and used this to great effect to keep a close control of the proceedings.

The PWG went on to be the driving force behind UNISON. It agreed the operating procedures, codified all the reporting schedules, and dealt with all the thorny issues relating to commission sharing. There was a huge amount of concern in New York that this group might start making decisions at a more junior level that should really be made by the partners, but in practice this never occurred. Problems were referred upwards in the best traditions of management – after they had been solved. What did emerge as the years went by was a group that was so close-knit that their allegiance to each other was in danger of being stronger than to their own colleagues. Above all, they all became firm friends.

The composition of the group, with the exception of the Dutch until Gert van de Sande came along, was surprisingly consistent. Bob Beane took over from Ken Seward for Italy, and was replaced at Gil y Carvajal by Javier Barcaiztegui; Christian Dahms was succeeded by Dietrich Schauff; on his retirement Ronnie Westhorp was succeeded by Ian Macalpine-Leny, Hugh Hausman and Henri Sommer by Claude Sautière when Claude took over the international department of Gras Savoye. Rudi Portaria, along of course with Dany Kervyn, continued on regardless.

The PWG in 1989: (from left) *Chip Bechtold, Ian Macalpine-Leny, Javier Barcaiztegui, Dany Kervyn, Gert van de Sande, Göran Groth, Claude Sautière, Dietrich Schauff, Martin Rayner*

By 1984 Bickett had been a director of J&H for five years, and it was time for him to hand over. The obvious choice was Bob Beane, who was then running Italy. In typical Bickett style, he started the meeting in the morning, but then announced he would join the partners' group at the coffee break and not return. Beane moved into Peter's seat and started on the next item on the agenda, but Javier Barcaiztegui was asleep, Ronnie Westhorp continued reading *The Times*, Dany Kervyn was busily looking at his files, Ian Macalpine-Leny was so hungover after the party in Mike Barrett's room the night before that he just looked himself, and poor Bob went redder, and redder and redder. Eventually, enough was enough, the point had been made, and the meeting resumed.

Because this group of individuals from different brokers and different nationalities worked so well together as a team, they were an obvious target for the Americans to turn into a production tool. So in 1979, a series of road shows were put together in New York, Philadelphia, Chicago and St Louis. After the formal presentations, when each member of the PWG spoke on a topic of particular relevance to their country, there was an open house, and everyone sat at an individual table with their national flag in the centre. When it came to Chicago there didn't seem to be many of the audience with Italian subsidiaries, so Ken Seward glanced across at the French table. Every woman who had attended the formal presentations had gathered round Claude Sautière. But what really sealed Claude's reputation was that when he came down into the lobby (last) to join the group prior to going out to dinner, the pianist immediately stopped playing and, shrieking 'Claude', rushed over and gave him the most enormous kiss. No one, of course, entirely believed his explanation.

Dinner was hosted by Mitch LaMotte, the director in charge of the Chicago office, who arrived wearing a seersucker jacket and a bow tie. 'Are you dressed for a costume party?' asked Herman Verbon of Mees & zoonen. The evening had not got off to an auspicious start. When they reached the restaurant, it was quite clear that all Mitch wanted to do was reminisce about old times in J&H Philadelphia with Bickett and Beane, which he did over several cocktails without ordering any wine for the Europeans. Finally, Christian Dahms prised the wine list out of him and, absolutely seething by this point, ordered two bottles of the most expensive red wine on the menu.

The bond between members of the PWG became so strong that it was unanimously decreed that Javier Barcaiztegui should ask formal permission before getting married. This of course was granted, at the meeting in Paris in February 1985. By way of celebration, Claude Sautière organised a memorable evening at the Crazy Horse. Much no doubt to his fiancée Lola's relief, Javier was struck down by a sudden stomach bug, and was too sick to attend.

If the annual conference epitomised the UNISON network, it was the PWG that crystallised it. Here was a group of different nationalities working for completely independent brokerage companies that became so closely united that they behaved as a virtual organisation. Reality can occasionally be one jump ahead of the drawing board.

12 The Search for a Brand

By the beginning of the 1980s the J&H international network had emerged as the leading brokerage network in terms of global service, but the wholly-owned competitors were forever snapping at its heels. One of the problems was that the concept was difficult to sell or, more exactly, to appreciate, until you had experienced it, like many of the best things in life. The competitors were forever pushing the fact that their networks were owned, and ownership equalled control. The J&H network needed a brand that would be the standard-bearer for the virtual organisation: clearly a subject for the PWG.

The PWG deliberated long and hard, but attempts to come up with some dreadful acronym failed. The ball was picked up by J&H New York, and Seth Faison was charged with coming up with a brand name. Seth had been hired by Dorrance Sexton in 1958 to develop sales training throughout the J&H system, and to help reorganise the corporate advertising. A cultured man of the old school, he invariably wore a seersucker suit in the summer, and a bow-tie. By the beginning of the 1980s he was chairman of the advertising committee. Seth set out to find a name that would be meaningful in any language, and a turn-

"THE MAN WHO HAD THE CHEAP SOLUTION FOR THE UNISON BOOTH"

off in none. One of the early suggestions was Aegis, a Greek word for the shield of Zeus, which means 'protection' in English, but it was soon discovered that this had already been taken by someone else. His next suggestion was UNISON, which gave a general impression of unity and togetherness. Peter Bickett sent this, like other possibilities, round the various correspondents, and no one terribly liked it. Time was drifting by, and after some twenty months no decision had been made. Eventually New York had had enough, and Bickett, who had been made the second international director in 1979, announced that in the absence of any progress, and with the blessing of most of the correspondents, the new brand name for the J&H international network was going to be UNISON.

At the next PWG meeting when the name came up for discussion, the French began to be awkward. Claude Sautière explained that in French it sounded like a musical note, which was not appropriate for a professional brokerage network. 'Perfect,' said Bickett. 'One note.' But Claude would not give up. 'Then it should be spelt UNISSON.' No, said Bickett, that was clearly ridiculous. Without saying a word, Javier Barcaiztegui reached into his pocket and placed on the table a packet of Spanish condoms proudly bearing the name 'Unison'. There was stunned silence. 'Protection,' said Bickett, clearly not to be deflected.

And so UNISON it became. As with all successful brands, whether 'The Beatles' or 'Rentokil' or 'Black & Decker', the actual meaning of the name is soon forgotten. It immediately becomes associated with the product, or pop group, or service, and becomes totally synonymous with it. So it was with UNISON. A logo was designed, which was rather tame compared with some of the alternatives produced by Javier Barcaiztegui, who always seemed to spend most of the meetings drawing, and all the correspondents became 'Partners in UNISON'. Here at last was something solid that all members of the network could display as part of their corporate advertising and on their business cards. It rapidly became the gold standard for international client servicing in the world of insurance.

While the name changed nothing about the way the network operated, it had a great effect on clients, markets and competitors. It seemed to them to be something more than it was – the co-ordinated efforts of a group of independent firms. This was particularly true in Europe when the concept of co-ordinated global insurance programmes emerged.

As all the world knows, insurance conventions are always held in exotic locations, otherwise no one goes. Monte Carlo, San Francisco, Rome, Baden-Baden – the list is endless, but never includes Manchester, Trenton, Essen or Turin. With the rise in

popularity of all types of conventions in the 1980s there appeared a new phenomenon, the Exhibition. This was where you could browse for hours along line after line of bored exhibitors attempting to flog their wares, with the sole intention of hoovering up as many free give-aways for your children as you could manage. As far as UNISON was concerned, the most important conference occurred every second year in October in Monte Carlo. At the 1983 conference, UNISON's little portable exhibition booth looked decidedly out of place when compared with the large aggressive display put on by arch-rival Marsh & McLennan. All agreed that UNISON must have something that would completely outclass the competition.

The PWG immediately got to work on the problem. The British suggested a very complicated display featuring maps and details of all the individual offices; the Spanish wanted to have a bar and serve wine; the French thought food should also be provided; the Dutch of course were worried about how much all this was going to cost. The possibilities were endless. In the end, it was decided to hire a consultant, who came up with some excellent ideas – at a price, needless to say. A very

simple design by a German company was selected, one that would never become out of date, and the Germans proceeded with the construction, embodying all the strength of materials and attention to detail that one might expect from them. It was stunning. It swept the board at Monte Carlo in 1985 and, manned by two of Javier Barcaiztegui's secret weapons ('manned' is probably the wrong word under the circumstances), it was guaranteed to be the centre of attraction. UNISON was once again supreme.

But such conferences only last three days, and this was a large investment. What other opportunities were there to use the booth? Willis had a large international conference for clients and prospects coming up in the Tower Room of Ten Trinity Square* the following January, so the booth was shipped to London in time for that event.† It created quite a stir in the lobby of Ten Trinity Square, but not exactly in the way envisaged. In an exhibition hall it's often difficult to gauge exactly

* Willis's head office, see p. 45
† Accompanied by two German technicians, without whom it was impossible to erect it.

how big such structures are. The lobby of Ten Trinity square is not exactly small, but the booth proved so large that the normal central entrance door (there are three) had to be closed, and everyone came into the building through the one on the left. The conference, needless to say, was a great success.

Transport back and forth from Monte Carlo turned out to cost an arm and a leg, so after the 1987 conference, Gras Savoye offered to arrange to have it stored in Monte Carlo. When the

1989 conference came round, it was discovered rather late in the day that the booth had somehow got fairly seriously damaged, and there were various parts missing. Someone had the bright idea of going out and buying various pots of flowers, to hide the damage. The UNISON booth for the 1989 conference would have done credit to London's annual Chelsea Flower Show.

One can't help wondering where it is today.

13 Foreigners in New York

As the 1970s took hold, the European business that J&H introduced to the network increased dramatically, and with it the
reputation of J&H as an international broker. But something
else was happening. The strength of the European currencies
against the dollar, particularly the pound, and more favourable
employment laws in the US ushered in an increasing trend of
investment into America, led by the British. What began as a
trickle soon became a flood as the Germans and even the French
piled in. All of a sudden, Willis and Jauch & Hübener found
themselves in the position of being able to introduce business to
J&H, what came to be known as 'Reverse Flow'. The Germans
were first in on the act, being much more organised, but Willis
soon caught up after a slow start.

It was quickly discovered that although the Americans were
extremely good at directing and controlling business going into
Europe, and had spent ten years laying down the law as to pre-
cisely how this should be done, it was a completely different
story when the boot was on the other foot. In part, the problem
was that the introduced accounts were looked after by domestic
account executives, who treated them as just another piece of
local business, because that's all they knew about. This of course
didn't happen with the outgoing J&H business, because with the
exception of Willis, all account executives handling international
business had to have an additional skill that set them apart from
their domestic colleagues – they had to be fluent in English.

Very soon, Jauch & Hübener saw the problem. About this
time one of their account executives who handled some of the
biggest J&H-introduced accounts in Germany, and had made
trips to the US to see General Motors and 3M, went to the US on
holiday. It was 1976, the year of the Bicentennial, and Dietrich
Schauff had a wonderful four-week trip. When he came back
he went straight to Ewald Lahno, the chairman of Jauch &
Hübener, and told him that what was needed to improve the
local service to German multinational clients in the US was to
base one of their people in J&H. 'But who could we send?' said

Lahno. 'You're looking at him,' said Schauff, never one to be shy. Immediately Lahno looked in his diary and arranged an evening for Dietrich to go round and see him at home. A plan was devised that Lahno subsequently sold to Oschi Hübener in such a way that Oschi always thought it was his idea in the first place. He and Dietrich always got on well – they shared the same birthday. As with everything the Germans did, this was planned with military precision. Dietrich had twelve months to hand over his accounts, during which time he moved to Frankfurt to take over as manager of the international department while Patrick Thomas* was in the US. In March 1979 Dietrich then moved to New York.

Claude Sautière was now in New York, nearing the end of his assignment to get to know J&H. Space was cramped on the twelfth floor of 95 Wall Street prior to international's move to the much more spacious ninth floor, so Dietrich and Claude had next-door desks in a little corridor separated by a partition, which soon became known as the Maginot Line. Every morning when Dietrich came in he said *'Bonjour, mon Général,'* to which Claude replied, *'Guten Morgen, mein Führer.'* The poor J&H-ers, not being used to this sort of thing, thought World War III was about to break out. Before he left, Claude Sautière did Dietrich a great turn by introducing him to his real-estate broker, Ellen Terhune. Ellen went on not only to find Dietrich's apartment but eventually, after a long chase,† to become Frau Schauff.

With Dietrich installed in J&H New York and Claude on his way back to Paris, it didn't take Gras Savoye long to decide that they also needed a representative with J&H. Thanks to the revolution in Iran, Luc Malâtre had had his two-year foreign assignment reduced to one, so once back in Paris he went to see Patrick Lucas to ask where he could spend the second. As it transpired, Patrick didn't have an answer up his sleeve, so Luc reminded him that as he was also a US citizen, it would be very easy to transfer to the US. So it was that in September 1979, Luc

* English manager of Jauch & Hübener's international department.
† Finally brought to an end when Dietrich learnt from Harald Hübener that it would be difficult to take up his next assignment, two years with Willis in South Africa, unless they were married.

ANOTHER CHEAP SOLUTION for MONTECARLO and ... the UNISON booth!

became the second foreign representative to be stationed in J&H New York.

By a quirk of fate, Luc had been born on 4 July in Pensacola, Florida, but was unquestionably French. He had joined Gras Savoye from a firm of management consultants in 1974, aged 21, to set up a risk management services capability. He then left to do his compulsory military service as attaché to the French Embassy in Somalia, during which time the French Ambassador had the misfortune to be kidnapped. By the time Luc returned, Gras Savoye had joined the J&H network, and he was given the task of being the first American-style account manager of a large French client – Rhône Poulenc. In early January 1978 he replaced Claude Sautière as manager in Tehran. He arrived on his first day in New York wearing an ivory pin-striped suit, black shirt and black tie, and those black see-through silk stockings worn by all aristocratic Frenchmen.

The job description of these foreign representatives was simple – to do whatever was necessary to assist J&H in winning and servicing the US subsidiaries of their company's clients. In Jauch & Hübener's case this immediately produced positive results, prompting Mike Faiers, always keen to play one broker off against another, to insist that Willis send someone out to sort out J&H's servicing of GKN's new US acquisitions.

Ian Macalpine-Leny was at the photocopier one day in Willis's head office at Ten Trinity Square when Tommy Thomson came out of his office. 'I want a word with you,' he said, so Ian followed him back wondering what on earth he had done wrong now. 'How would you like to go and work with J&H in New York for three years?' 'I would like to very much,' Ian replied. 'Don't be so bloody silly, go away and think about it,' came the reply. 'I don't need to,' Ian said. 'The answer's yes.' Thomson slowly banged out his pipe in his glass ashtray. 'Got any dependants?' Thus it was that six months later, in June 1980, Ian joined Dietrich and Luc in New York.

Thomson admitted that he couldn't give Ian much advice because he didn't know what the job would involve, so, knowing that Michael Day had been there twenty years before, Ian went down to see him. 'As you know, sir, I'm being sent to J&H

David Slade

New York for three years, and I was wondering if you could give me any advice, apart of course from getting my hair cut.' 'Yes,' said Michael. 'Brush it.' The only other worthwhile advice came from David Slade, 'Pongo' to the Lloyd's community: 'Keep your mouth closed and your bowels open.' It was difficult to argue with that.

Arriving in New York, Ian reported to Rudi Portaria who, having returned from Brussels the year before, was now responsible for the 'reverse flow' business. 'What are we going to call you?' said Rudi. 'What's wrong with Ian Macalpine-Leny?' Ian replied. Clearly this wasn't the answer expected.* Rudi next

* He was known as 'Hyphen' by the domestic people in J&H New York.

explained that the secretary looking after the three foreign reps was Michael Steele. Much to Ian's relief, Michael turned out to be a very bright and attractive young lady with red hair. 'How do you want your filing set up?' she asked Dietrich on his first day. 'Don't worry about the filing,' came back the reply. 'Just fetch the coffee.' Michael proved to be the most excellent secretary until she was lured away by Jim Harlow* some two years later to fill a wider role.

The first problem facing the foreigners was how to treat each other's national holidays. This was solved by Dietrich who, being the oldest and most experienced of the three, quickly emerged as the unofficial shop steward. 'We'll observe all of them,' he said, and so it was. They were joined later in the summer by Takeo Hoshine, a Japanese from J&H Tokyo with uncharacteristically aggressive business habits for a Japanese. Takeo brought a new twist. His diary carried a little bit of narrative every day that explained whether the day in question was a good or a bad day to do things. It was unclear whether he acted on it, but he always consulted it. Takeo's lifelong ambition had been to own a Cadillac, and it was one he wasted no time in fulfilling. Being rather small, he had to sit on a series of cushions, and then could only drive peering through the steering wheel. Reversing, of course, was out of the question.

Having resident representatives from Jauch & Hübener, Gras Savoye and Willis in New York presented a great sales opportunity for J&H, who lost no time in wheeling them out to be introduced to clients and prospective clients. But if J&H thought they had three tame foreigners on someone else's payroll, they were in for a rude awakening. All three reacted quickly and strongly to any inefficiency or incompetence on the part of the US servicing team. Dietrich in particular was especially blunt, and many a young account executive lived in fear of him. Tall and imposing with a stern expression and piercing eyes which hid a wonderful sense of humour, he would have many a J&H-er quaking in their boots. 'I was not sent here to win a beauty competition,' he would say. Just as well, they no doubt thought.

* The director who became the first managing director of the newly created New York branch; see p. 129

Ian knew nothing about international insurance when he arrived from London, but he learned quickly. He also learned that Americans liked their Brits to be caricatures of the British and, being a natural extrovert, had no intention of disappointing them. Addressing his first production meeting in pinstriped suit, blue-and-white striped shirt, old school tie and red braces (suspenders), he ensured that his audience would listen to his message by announcing that he had 'a sense of humour, a hide like a rhinoceros, and wasn't nearly as stupid as he looked'. The Americans loved it.

Travelling on his first business trip to St Louis, Ian checked in to his hotel and asked if they had a reservation for Ian Macalpine-Leny. 'Oh yes, sir,' said the helpful receptionist. 'We have one for Mr Macalpine and one for Mr Leny.' Those were the days when a copy of the *Financial Times* was a rare sight in the US, and Ian initially had them sent out by courier. He would then take any unread copies on his next trip, and catch up with them on the plane. 'Is that a very old newspaper?' asked the man in the next seat, obviously thinking its pink colour was due to the effects of time.

Some months after arriving in New York, Dietrich made a trip to Toronto to call on the Canadian subsidiaries of some German clients. All went well till the return journey, when an officious little Puerto Rican immigration man (US immigration is dealt with in Toronto) noticed Dietrich's tourist visa, and a search of his briefcase revealed all his business files. Clearly he was not on a pleasure trip, and he was not allowed to re-enter the US. Brian Jones was a little surprised to see him back in the Toronto office the next morning, especially as he was looking (for Dietrich) a little crumpled – all his checked luggage was by now safely in New York. Well, this was a Friday, so Dietrich spent a productive, if crumpled, day making further calls, while the telephone wires between Toronto, New York and Mülheim were kept very busy. At the end of the day, the ever-hospitable Jones invited Dietrich to stay the weekend at his cottage on Lake Muskoka.

The following day, Saturday, Dietrich was invited by a friend of Brian's to go on a boat trip across the lake, and having taken the precaution of loading a couple of crates of beer, they set off. 6 p.m. came, and then 7 p.m., and by 8 p.m. it was getting dark, but they still had not returned. At 9.30 p.m., Brian received a call from another friend to say he had picked up a May Day call from the boat saying they had run out of gas and beer, and could the Jones cottage be advised and a rescue launched. Brian immediately set off and eventually found the boat. By this time they had been without beer for three hours, and had drifted in to within a hundred yards of the shore. Thus began the firm friendship between Brian Jones and Dietrich Schauff. It was ten days before a judge in Buffalo over-ruled the immigration official and Dietrich was allowed back into the US.

If you were only going to meet one Canadian, that Canadian should be Brian Jones. The son of a chief executive of rival brokers Tomenson, Saunders, Whitehead, Brian joined J&H Willis Faber in 1976 as executive assistant to the president and rose to become managing director. With a heart of extremely large proportions, a fanatical interest in fishing and duck hunting and an incredible capacity for work, he is the most wonderful company, and has a natural gift for talking to anyone. Once in Manhattan he persuaded a limo* driver to take his entire family on a double or quits basis: twice the agreed fare or for free, depending on the outcome. Brian won the toss.

One of the early bits of advice Dietrich gave Ian was to check whether his job description said 'USA' or 'North America'. As it hadn't yet been drawn up, this was a relatively simple matter to fix, and Ian was soon on the first of many trips to Toronto, where he too became a close friend of Brian Jones. The first time they ever met there were several drinks in the Chateau Bar & Grill across the street from the office in New York, followed by a ride up-town with Dietrich. Unfortunately there was some hold up en route and Ian ended by getting out and having a pee on the FDR Drive, much to the amusement of the other commuters.

Ian was instructed by Willis to penetrate J&H at all levels, an instruction, incidentally, he did not take literally, but he soon developed a reputation for giving very good parties in his apartment. This was an excellent way of introducing clients and

* As limousines are ubiquitously called in the USA.

visiting Willis people, and thanking those that had worked hard on Willis accounts. Soon after Martin Kessler arrived in New York in the summer of 1980, he came to see Ian in the morning to thank him for the party the previous night. 'Ian,' he said, in the strong Swiss-German accent he had when he first arrived, 'I have learnt a new word: "Hang Over".'

In the days before e-mail there was a great deal more reliance on the telephone, with all the attendant time shift problems when calling from Europe. One night Ian was vaguely aware of a phone ringing miles away in his dreams, but it suddenly became a reality.

'Yes?' he said, managing to locate the receiver in the dark.

'Thomson.'

'Who?'

'Thomson.'

'I'm sorry, who did you say?'

'THOMSON!'

By this time Ian had managed to get the light on and look at the clock.

'Whatever's the matter? – it's 4.30 in the morning.'

'Were you asleep?' said Tommy Thomson, never at a loss for a quick response.

The other thing that was difficult for people in Europe to get their heads round was the sheer size of the USA. Dowty had made an acquisition of a new company in Yakima, Washington State, and as they were a very important client of Willis's, George O'Neill, the managing director of Willis's UK retail company, rang Ian to ask if he would go over and see them straight away. 'That's very timely,' said Ian, 'because I've got a trip to Seattle planned next week.' 'Why can't you go tomorrow?' came the reply. 'Well,' said Ian, 'it's a five-hour flight followed by a hundred-and-fifty mile car journey.' There was silence on the other end of the phone. Clearly it hadn't looked that far on the map. Ian will never forget that car journey. About halfway, in the middle of nowhere, he saw some road works on the horizon. When he got up to them, the man operating the Stop/Go sign wore a Frankenstein mask. It was Hallowe'en.

The resident reps frequently found themselves being invited

to speak to business or insurance groups. On being invited to address the Palo Alto RIMS (Risk and Insurance Management Society) chapter on '1992',* Ian Macalpine-Leny thought that he ought to find out what 1992 meant to the majority of insurance people in northern California. Dick Wilson, Hewlett Packard's risk manager, thought for a moment and then said, 'The five-hundredth anniversary of the arrival of Christopher Columbus.'

By 1982 the reps from Jauch & Hübener, Gras Savoye and Willis had been joined by Arnold Klapwijk from Mees & zoon-en. Arnold proved to be an excellent choice, and together with his charming wife Susan had a very successful assignment. The original foreign reps were succeeded by others, some more successful than others, but none more so than Corinna Kratz of Jauch & Hübener. One of the very few Germans with a broad Texas accent and a beer consumption that many a man would be proud of, she brought a no-nonsense approach to business production. And she loved to party. But the cost of maintaining foreign reps in New York was high. Even Claude Sautière finally realised that he could make endless Concorde trips for the price of maintaining a permanent Gras Savoye post there.

The incoming American business did much more than provide a useful source of additional income to both the producing broker and J&H; it served to closely lock the UNISON network together as business started to flow in both directions. This was increasingly followed by exchange of business between all the UNISON partners as British, German, French, Dutch and other multinational companies became clients of UNISON.

But for the lucky few who had the key job of being resident representatives in New York, this was a fantastic opportunity which totally changed their careers. As Ian Macalpine-Leny was to remark so many times afterwards, he had the best job in Willis. He had a staff of one, namely himself; his territory was the whole of North America; and his boss, Adrian Gregory, was three thousand six hundred miles away. It doesn't get much better than that.

* The introduction of the Freedom of Services directive in the European Community in 1992.

14 The Death of Lunchtime O'Booze*

On 11 May 1982 there occurred an event so momentous that the repercussions were felt throughout the entire insurance world: J&H banned drinking at lunchtime. Lunchtime drinking had long been a feature of the brokerage world in New York, and there, as in London, considerable business was done over a glass or two. But it followed a different pattern to its London equivalent. Whereas the Lloyd's broker would go out and have a couple of gin and tonics, or even a pint of 'London Pride' or 'Old Speckled Hen' before settling down to a good bottle of wine with lunch, the New York broker would have three large dry Martinis followed by a completely dry lunch. Ian Macalpine-Leny always found the latter particularly difficult because he had to have a glass of something to help him swallow. As the New York Martinis were pretty much neat gin, their effect was not inconsiderable.

As might be expected, there was the occasional culprit in all areas of the firm. Ward Chase wasn't the only director who wasn't much good in the afternoons, and even the General was no slouch in that department. So Dick Purnell brought in a rule that directors should not drink at lunchtime, whatever the situation and whoever the company, in part to set an example to the rest. It was strictly adhered to.

At the time of the proposed merger between Dunlop & Pirelli, Willis and J&H Italy were competing against C. T. Bowring† for the property damage and business interruption business. Willis had succeeded in introducing quite a few of their senior people to the new management, so Ken Seward thought he would take advantage of a visit by Dick Purnell to Milan to introduce him to Adalberto Castagna, Pirelli's corpo-

* For the benefit of those who don't read *Private Eye*, 'Lunchtime O'Booze' is an entirely fictitious Fleet Street journalist, although several of the real-life members of that tribe claim to be the original role model.
† Major UK broker subsequently acquired by Marsh & McLennan.

128

rate secretary. Ken arranged lunch in a very special restaurant which was a great success, as Purnell and Castagna hit it off immediately. The first bottle of *Pinot Grigio* soon disappeared, and Seward, ever the perfect host, ordered another. At this point, Purnell thought he should say something. 'You know, Adalberto, in New York I don't drink at lunch, and don't allow my partners to do so either.' 'But Deeeck,' said Castagna, 'this is not drinking, this is part of lunch.' 'I guess you're right,' said Purnell, taking another sip of wine. After that Seward never worried about drinking wine in Milan.

One of the changes Bob Hatcher brought in when he took over from Purnell at the beginning of 1982 was to create a separate New York branch office, and appointed Jim Harlow, one of the New York directors, to run it. Like many employee benefits people, Harlow was an unusual fellow. He attacked everything with a missionary zeal, scheduling staff meetings to begin at 7.30 a.m. After working an exceptionally hard day he would always be an enthusiastic party-er in the evening. Then there he was again, bright-eyed and bushy-tailed at 7 a.m. the next morning.

Harlow believed that every effort must be made to increase J&H productivity, and as drinking at lunchtime clearly reduced post-prandial effectiveness, and had long been banned for the directors, it had to go. He readily got the backing of Hatcher to extend the ban, hence the famous memo that landed on the desks of the unsuspecting employees one Tuesday morning. It didn't take long for the press to get hold of it. Liz Smith, the gossip columnist of the *Daily News*, picked up the story, and ran it on her 'Alive at Five' television show. Then the other stations picked it up. Lunchtime the next day saw them all camped outside 95 Wall Street, and following sombre-looking J&H-ers to lunch. Others staked out nearby hostelries, waiting for the J&H-ers to arrive, and had a wonderful time interviewing funpoking rivals. Jim Harlow was interviewed on TV that evening and explained that he got just as much pleasure out of having a glass of Perrier with his lunch. Not being used to getting free advertising from such an unlikely source, a grateful Perrier company sent crates of the stuff to Harlow's office. 'Johnson &

Higgins bars wet lunches for its employees – staid insurance broker's sober ruling could discomfort some clients, rivals say' ran the headline in the *Wall Street Journal*. Seth Faison was kept busy, knowing that there is no such thing as bad publicity.

The foreign reps, needless to say, simply went on regardless. Any European guest would have been most put out not to be offered a drink at lunchtime, even more so if his host didn't join him. Meanwhile the local bars were doing a roaring trade in 'J&H Cocktails' – a glass of neat vodka on the rocks with a twist, and an empty bottle of Perrier.

As so often was the case, the last word was had by Emil Kratovil. Kratovil was a friend of Sexton's from the navy, whom Sexton persuaded to join J&H. Now coming to the end of his career, he picked up his pen and wrote the following:

The Ballad of Water and Wall

There are strange things done, 'neath the mid-day sun,
At the corner of Water and Wall,
And that cynical joker, the Oldest Broker,
Who's cursed with total recall,
Says that May the eleventh of eighty-two,
Was the day that was darkest of all.

He remembers them well: the mournful knell
That Black Friday tolled o'er the Street,
December the seventh of 'forty-one, when we lost our
    Pacific Fleet.
But the worst day yet, he's prepared to bet,
(And one can't see how he can lose),
Was that tragic day, in the month of May,
When J&H banned the booze.

There were moans of anguish and screams of rage
When the word came down from on high.
From the poshest club and the seediest pub
Could be heard a regretful sigh.
And we wondered, what was the final straw
That made J&H go dry?

130

It's not the Directors who brought this on,
The Oldest Broker sighed,
It'd cost them two hundred grand a year
To be seen in public, fried.
I suspect that the habit has trickled down,
And the leaks can be seen, outside.

Now it's not very nice when a private vice
Is exposed to the public view,
And the Grand Old Firm was beginning to squirm
When it learned what the public knew.
Indecent exposure was worse for them
Than it would be for me, or for you.

Avast there, below! All hands man the pumps!
Cried the swaggering CEO,
We'll soon have the driest galley afloat:
The rumpots have got to go—
or I'll know the reason why! he said,
Send a memo down below!

Now weep for those pitiful galley-slaves,
A most abstemious bunch.
Their street had become a wailing Wall, and
Thanks to the management crunch,
In memory alone survives
The three-Martini lunch.

The alphabet brokers are having a ball,
The Oldest Broker reports,
A&A, C&B, FBH, M&M
Are convinced this game is for sports;
They know what impossible deals have been done
With the help of a couple of snorts.

So shed a few tears for a brokerage firm
Which has brought on itself the suspicion
That its clients were served by a staff which was not,

As a rule, in a sober condition.
Said the Oldest Broker, You'd think they'd have learned
That no one respects Prohibition.
And these were the final words he said
As he staggered out the door.
The Moral Majority won the day–
But J&H lost the war!

Emil A Kratovil
With due and proper obeisance to
Robert William Service

Dick Nijhoff

15 The Unsung Heroes

The original concept of the partners in UNISON applied only to Europe, but such was the success of the brand that it was an obvious progression to extend it worldwide. So each J&H overseas office, some of them somewhat reluctantly because it didn't appear to them to be necessary, became the UNISON partner for their particular country. The tale of how some of these offices came into being is well worth telling.

Ironically, the operation that most closely followed the UNISON goal of a jointly owned company was set up five years before UNISON came into being. United Iranian Insurance Services was a joint venture between Willis, J&H, Jauch & Hübener and Mahmoud Zand, whose company, Zand Insurance Offices, was the leading broker in Iran. The company opened for business in Tehran in May 1977. Willis already had major reinsurance business with the two leading Iranian insurance companies, and both J&H and Jauch & Hübener had clients rushing to take advantage of the Iranian oil boom.

As a reward for the incredible job that Hugh Hausman had done in managing the transfer of J&H's French business from SGCA to Gras Savoye, Lloyd Benedict relocated him to Tehran.* If Hugh had been an object of fun in Paris, he was absolutely hilarious in Tehran. His main form of recreation was drinking gin and tonic by the pool watching Eugen Kronberger's lovely wife in her bikini. Kronberger, who was Jauch & Hübener's representative, was one of those incredible people who are both absolute genius and complete and utter idiot. Christian Dahms has never recovered from getting Kronberger on the speakerphone one Friday afternoon during the end-of-week winddown with his international team. As the possibility of revolution became more and more likely, Kronberger had succeeded in getting a forty per cent 'lead line' from the AIU (American International Underwriters) for a strikes, riots &

---

* The assignment had originally been offered to George Rainoff, but after all the trouble and disruption that they had suffered in the Lebanon (see p. 140), his wife didn't want to go.

civil commotion cover for terrorist activities and was absolutely convinced that a fortune could be made if Jauch & Hübener could place the remaining sixty per cent. In addition to his wife, his other great asset was his dachshund. With foreigners flying out of Tehran in droves in January 1979, Herr Kronberger was seen flying in from holiday, *mit* dachshund.

The unlikely trio of foreign nationals was completed by Tony South, the manager from Willis. Tony's principal requirement on being offered the job was a Range Rover as his company car, which Willis duly provided. Tony was a most engaging character, but office systems were not his strong suit, and things got in such a mess that a young man from Willis's Sheffield office, Peter Crawford, was flown in for three weeks to sort it out. Peter had never been outside the UK before, so the whole thing was an absolute eye-opener to him, particularly as there was no alphabetical filing system, and the staff could speak English but not read it. With great presence of mind he dispatched a member of staff down to the bazaar to buy ring binders and a four-hole punch, and in next to no time the Tehran office not only had a filing system, all colour-coded in accordance with the Sheffield system, but was issuing debit notes and credit notes as well. What's more, they even had a client list. The only member of staff who did know what was going on and who spoke excellent English was Abid Kermani, who was subsequently transferred to the US and had a very successful career with J&H in New York and Detroit.

France had always been a major investor in Iran, and Gras Savoye had set up their own office in Tehran in 1975. Luc Malâtre had taken over as manager from Claude Sautière in 1978, but by the end of the year, with foreign businesses pulling out every day, Luc closed his office and took space in the offices of United Iranian Insurance Services. After Ayatollah Khomeini returned at the beginning of February 1979, Luc sent his family back to Paris, and he and Hugh Hausman spent a lot of time together, becoming firm friends. Despite everything disintegrating around them, Hugh was completely unfazed, only losing his cool when Peter Bickett called him up on some minor point of administration. 'God damn it!' he said holding the telephone out of the window. 'Can't you hear? – they're shooting people out there.' Both Hugh and Luc eventually got home unscathed. Tehran was the only UNISON office where you were guaranteed to be given caviar for lunch, so its closure was a pity.

J&H's representation in Tokyo did not exactly get off to an auspicious start. There wasn't a lot to choose from, so a correspondent relationship was set up with Aurell Brokerage Inc. The first introduced client arrived in Tokyo to be met with the naïve suggestion that it would be much easier if they forgot about J&H and dealt direct with Aurell. So that relationship didn't last very long. At about this time a new broker emerged in Tokyo called International Insurance Inc. whose president, David Maul, was a former soft drinks salesman. His lack of insurance experience seemed to be offset by his aggressiveness in business and his ability to hire very good technical people. His firm was also given some stature by its chairman, a Mr Wideman (*sic*), who had an important position with Union Carbide in the Far East. As there wasn't much choice, J&H entered into a correspondent agreement with David Maul's firm.

There wasn't much introduced business in the mid 1960s, but what there was seemed to be handled satisfactorily. In the autumn of 1967, Dorrance Sexton had the first opportunity to meet David Maul (and his wife 'Tinklebell', who had three white poodles and one black, all on gold leads) when he spent a few days in their offices in New York.* Apart from his slightly flamboyant personality, there was nothing to cast any doubt on his capabilities until he announced that the main purpose of the trip was to ask J&H for a loan of half a million dollars. His business had been so successful that he wanted to open in Korea, Taiwan, Hong Kong, and several more places besides. Explaining that they were brokers not bankers, Sexton sent him back to Tokyo empty-handed. Apparently even this rather optimistic request didn't raise any eyebrows, so it was something of a shock when J&H learned early in 1968 that David Maul had been jailed by the Japanese.

* They stayed in a suite in the Plaza Hotel, where the poodles had room service.

It subsequently transpired that Maul's method of getting business was to entertain somewhat lavishly at various Japanese hot-spots, and it was even rumoured that on one occasion he bought a fur coat for the wife of a visiting US treasurer. As his business couldn't support this, he had, among other things, extended a large insurance policy for the Singer Manufacturing Company without informing the insurance company or, for that matter, passing on the premium. Fortunately Singer was not a J&H client at the time, but it did not look very good that J&H had been introducing clients to a correspondent whose president was now in jail for fraud.*

Salvation came from an unlikely quarter. George Rainoff had worked in Tokyo for the Insurance Company of North America for five years. On returning to New York in 1961 with passable Japanese he ended up working for the Factory Mutuals, but with the help of Charlie Anthony got an interview with J&H. Eight minutes into the interview with the General, he was told, 'You're coming, when can you start?' The year was 1965.

When the Maul problem broke in December 1967, Rainoff received a call from Dorrance Sexton to come and see him. 'Get on an airplane and go and see what needs to be done,' he was told. On his return, he recommended to Henshaw that J&H open their own office in Tokyo as the only practical option available. 'It seems you've manoeuvred yourself into a job,' said Sexton. Opening an office in Japan for a foreign company was no simple matter, but Sexton sought the help of an old friend who had been a trainee with J&H in the 1930s, Kenzo Misuzawa, who had risen to be chairman of the Tokio Marine, the largest Japanese insurance company. Two weeks later the licence had been obtained, and the Rainoffs were en route for Japan. George soon discovered that Tommy Kawamura, who had originally spilled the beans about David Maul's exploits to

* He was jailed for negotiating a loan from a prominent bank using Sumitomo 3M's three-year property premium as collateral. He later got out of jail and absconded to Hong Kong. He was last seen getting off the ferry holding hands with a diminutive young Hong Kong lady (he was at least 250lb and 6ft 3 in). For several years afterwards, a frequent topic among the old Tokyo and Hong Kong hands was 'whatever happened to David Maul?'

the Department of Finance, was an excellent man who had taken all the vital records home from the office. Together with a couple of other key employees, J&H Japan opened for business in April 1968. By the autumn of 1972 when George handed over to Hal Reynolds, J&H Japan was a thriving operation of forty-five to fifty people. The third *gaijin* was Mike Heim, who was on his first overseas posting. He and his wife Janie stopped off in San Francisco en route for Tokyo, and were taken out to a Polynesian restaurant by Rudi Portaria, who happened to be in town. Janie, being totally unfamiliar with foreign food and customs, was reassured when Mike told her that Rudi was the international expert, and all she needed to do was follow exactly what he did. So she struggled with her chopsticks, and when Rudi dipped something in the plum sauce, so did Janie; when Rudi added horseradish to his soy sauce, so did Janie; and when Rudi smeared sauce on his egg roll and picked it up to eat it, so did Janie – only to discover, at the same time as Rudi, that it was a hot towel.

When Charlie Binford took over as country manager in Japan in 1985 he tried, as he did for each of the subsequent nine years, to get a covered parking space in the garage under the J&H offices in Aoyama 1chome. It was explained to him through an interpreter that the J&H manager had to have the parking place out on the street next to the sidewalk, and he had to be able to back in so he could get away fast. Eventually, after about four years, it was explained to him that Peter Skov, one of his predecessors, had convinced the building manager that in addition to working for J&H he was also employed by the CIA, and there were times when he might have to make a fast getaway. He could not risk being in the underground parking garage and not able to get his car out in the event of a power failure. Nothing could change that story, and Binford's successor inherited the same parking spot. Peter Skov really did work for the CIA. He was hired by Lloyd Benedict at a job fair for retiring government employees. He was never without a black brief-case, which he even took to the men's room. He was known throughout J&H as 'the Spook'.

Skov was succeeded in 1983 by Martin Rayner. Born in South

Africa, married to a German, Hildegarde, he considered himself every bit the internationalist. He joined J&H in 1972 and rose to become manager of the highly successful international department in Los Angeles. He returned to New York in 1985 and was elected to the board in 1987 together with Bob Beane, and eventually took over from him as chairman of the PWG. He was particularly close to the Europeans, who all regarded him as a strong supporter and friend. He died suddenly in 1994 shortly after transferring from New York to Salt Lake City, aged fifty-six.

The first year that Binford was in Tokyo, his secretary came to him one day to say that the men had come to test the fire escape device in the mysterious box behind his desk. One man appeared who was obviously the boss, looking immaculate in his white overalls, followed by a bedraggled, dishevelled specimen who appeared to be on the verge of exhaustion. His overalls were filthy from top to bottom. They unpacked the equipment from the box, opened the window, and the boss nodded to his companion, who responded by putting his foot in a sling and jumping out the window. Binford dashed to the window expecting to see the wretched fellow splattered all over the sidewalk, instead of which he glided down the nine floors to a comfortable and safe landing. The boss-man stood to attention until the little man arrived at the J&H floor via the elevator, and then hurried over to the window. The contraption was reeled in and it was explained that the whole procedure had to be carried out twice, so the little man, who by this time was barely functioning, had to jump out of the window again. Calculating that the little guy who jumped out of the window weighed all of one hundred and twenty pounds and he was nearer two hundred and thirty-five, Binford thought he would ask a couple of questions. 'What do you think will happen when I put my foot in the sling and jump out of the window?' The boss-man got the question from Saito-san, Charlie's secretary, and sucked his teeth for at least a minute before he answered. Saito giggled. 'He said you go down very fast,' she translated.

By 1972 Lloyd Benedict had decided that J&H needed to open up in Singapore, and who better than George Rainoff who had made such a success in Japan? On calling in to see the insurance commissioner in Singapore to pay his respects, Rainoff was given two bits of advice: don't take insurance business out of the country unless you have to (he never did so without notifying the commissioner in advance), and don't pay any attention to the British and their silly tariff. George found both bits of advice invaluable. He was joined by Joseph T. Dell, who despite having a difficult time because his wife simply couldn't adjust to life in Singapore was an outstanding addition to the office, and later by Ed Dowd, who took over from Rainoff in 1974.

Ed Dowd's posting to Singapore was a bit unusual. He had joined J&H in Los Angeles in 1967; after an initial spell in the property department, he was asked to start the international department. Responding to the international expansion of both North American Aviation (subsequently part of Rockwell) and Litton Industries, Dowd and Bill Neidecker, president of the AIG on the West Coast, devised global all-risk property and transportation programmes. In addition to the breadth of cover, what really impressed clients was that the premium could be collected in any currency and paid to the AIG in Los Angeles with local servicing being carried out by the AIU, the AIG's international affiliate. These policies came to be designated 'B' accounts. It wasn't long before Dowd and his 'B' accounts began to seriously irritate the European correspondents, who were expected to provide local servicing on the other low-income lines of insurance while the majority of the income was sent back to Los Angeles. After receiving yet another complaint, Purnell lost his patience (not a rare occurrence) and told Benedict, 'Get him the hell out of LA. Send him as far away from LA as you can.' So this was how transfers were made. A good thing for Dowd that there wasn't a Boulevard Dowd in Moscow.

Joe Dell was the regional account executive, which involved a lot of travel, including regular trips to Indonesia every six weeks. On one such trip he flew from Jakarta to Surubaya in West Java to visit the Philip Morris plant at Malang. He was met by the Philip Morris driver, a very funny man who was always laughing and smiling, and smoked the local brand of clove-

139

scented tobacco made by his employer. It wasn't long before they came to a stop in a long line of vehicles, all with horns blaring and drivers yelling. The driver got out and walked up ahead to see what was going on. Moments later he returned laughing, motioning Joe to follow him. The sight that greeted him was one that he would never forget. A giant twelve-foot crocodile was lying across the two-lane road, mouth wide open and tail swinging as he was prodded by local police constables with long bamboo poles. Joe was simply terrified but everyone else thought it was great entertainment. At dinner that night, all the Philip Morris people were beside themselves with laughter. It seemed they had all been held up by that particular crocodile from time to time.

By the time he was back in New York, George Rainoff had established quite a reputation as a man who could be sent anywhere to open anything. His next assignment was to try and figure out what was happening in the Middle East, and how J&H could best take advantage of it. George thought the best thing to do was to go out and live in the region for a couple of years, so he accepted office space from Georges Assouad, general manager of the Willis office in Beirut. Willis Faber Middle East had been set up in 1973 in partnership with Middle East Airlines, a long-standing Willis client, and the Intra Investment Corporation. But by 1975 it was a very different story, with the whole area spiralling into civil war. George had been warned by someone in the marine department in New York that there was trouble brewing in Lebanon and this was not the time to move to Beirut with his family, but in typical fashion had brushed this aside. 'Damn domestic types – what do they know about things international?' Arriving in August to move into his rented flat, he found the whole place a war zone. Even Rainoff knew defeat when he saw it, so after six weeks he and his wife Carol moved back to Athens. The ten-block taxi ride to the offices of Middle East Airlines cost fifty dollars and then it was out to the airport in the crew bus, its sides armour-plated. Breakfast on the flight to Athens consisted of a litre of Black Label Scotch whisky for each passenger.

The problem was his shipment of furniture and personal

effects. This was already en route, but had been held up in Yugoslavia. He did everything he could to have it stopped, but the German transit company had been paid to ship a container to Beirut, so to Beirut it was going to go. Now, whereas Hugh Hausman had spent more than fifteen years working overseas and never collected anything other than the matches from numerous restaurants and some coat checks that he had forgotten to reclaim, George Rainoff had a wonderful collection of antiques together with his stamp collection and his wife's priceless collection of small Imari dishes. He had to find that container.

In true Rainoff style, George discovered a Lebanese playboy called Sabah Nader who agreed to take him back to Beirut. The arrangement was that they would meet on the Athens flight to Limassol. Sabah duly came on board at the last minute, kissed all the stewardesses, and filled the rest of the first class section with his entourage. When they reached the port area of Limassol, Sabah's yacht turned out to be a small ship, the most memorable feature of which was a king-size bed in the main cabin. Stores of every conceivable nature were being loaded on board, under the watchful eye of two henchmen brandishing sub-machine-guns.

The following day a French–Lebanese friend of Sabah's called Robert showed up and invited them for lunch on board his forty-foot yacht. In addition to the captain, there were two gorgeous French women on board who were stretched out on the foredeck, 'stark bollock naked' to use George's own words. When it came to lunch, these women turned out to be the waitresses, and had dressed for the occasion with strategically placed napkins. The eyes of the Lebanese were on stalks.

When they docked in Beirut there was a large reception committee waiting to greet Sabah, complete with his brand-new silver BMW. No one would have known there was a war raging just down the road. Sadly, when George got ashore, he realised that it was hopeless – there were thousands of containers stacked in the port. To cheer him up, Sabah invited him to join them for dinner, the only American in a large gathering of Christian Lebanese. Several of the guests arrived in battle dress complete with automatic rifles, and just went into a bedroom to change as if nothing out of the ordinary was going on. Two things always stuck in George's mind about that dinner: the 1966 Château Lafite Rothschild ran out, and he sat next to a French-Lebanese who was being transferred to the World Bank in Washington, DC. His wife didn't want to go with him because she was afraid of the crime in Washington.

After this debacle Rainoff was based in Athens and then Rome, before moving to Paris in 1978 to take over when Hugh Hausman moved to Tehran. In 1981 he returned to New York to be responsible for the Middle East and Far East. From here he made frequent trips to Saudi Arabia trying to figure out how best J&H could open up in that country. The stories of these trips are legendary, for George couldn't travel anywhere without leaving something behind. One one occasion he discovered that he didn't have a visa to enter the country. 'Where's my visa?' he asked his secretary back in New York, as soon as he could find a phone. 'Oh, don't worry about your Visa, Mr Rainoff,' came back the helpful reply. 'Just use your American Express.'

J&H ended up opening their own office in Saudi. The first manager was John Swarbrick, a Brit, who had the misfortune to get hit by a taxi in Riyadh, and eventually had to be invalided back to New York for medical treatment. He was replaced by Bill Waters, a domestic insurance specialist from the Chicago office, who was the only internal applicant. He only lasted a couple of months, and is best remembered as the only man who went out in the desert wearing Gucci shoes. He in turn was replaced by Glenn Camp in 1984. On the first day in the job, Steve Lecky was taking Glenn around and managed to go through a red light, right in front of a police car. The traffic policeman pulled them over and took Steve's driving licence and *Iqama* (local papers), and said in the only English he knew, 'Follow me.'

Steve Lecky started saying, 'I'm going to jail, I'm going to jail.' 'You've got to be kidding,' said Camp. He wasn't. They arrived at the police station, he was sentenced on the spot to three days in jail, and promptly locked up. So there was one less person at Glenn Camp's 'Welcome aboard' party that night. Later on they took Steve some Kentucky Fried Chicken, a newspaper, and some toilet paper. You had to supply your own in the Al Khobar jail. Camp's first phone call back to New York was to report that they had someone in jail. Not a very good start.

Visiting Saudi Arabia not long after a minor stroke, George Rainoff was going with Glenn Camp from Al Khobar to Jeddah and then on to Riyadh on a three-day trip. Glenn drove to the hotel, picked up George, had the bellman put his bag in the boot of the car, and set off for the airport. Noting that George was having problems with his right arm, Glenn parked in front of the terminal and summoned a skycap. He gave the skycap his own bag and George's, and gave George his ticket so he could check them both in. He then went and parked the car and came back to the terminal with his briefcase.

When he got back to the terminal, George had checked them both in and they proceeded to the departure area. They had an uneventful flight to Jeddah, going over some work on the way. They got off the plane and went to collect their bags. Only three people were waiting for luggage. George's came up, the other guy's came up, and Glenn's didn't. They stood there for a few minutes and then George turned to Glenn and said, 'What are we waiting for?'

'My luggage,' said Glenn.

'You had luggage?'

'Yes, it was on the same trolley at Al Khobar.'

'That was yours?' said George very seriously. 'I saw it, but told the guy to take it away, it wasn't mine.'

Trying not to scream, Glenn said, 'George, what do you think? I am going on a three-day trip with no luggage? You think I have my briefs in my brief case?'

George, not at all nonplussed, said, 'Call the office in Khobar, someone can send it over for you. Let's go.'

On one occasion George left his car at the train station in New Jersey, and on returning, sure enough, couldn't find his keys. Reaching his car, he found a note asking him to go to the police station. Having produced identification and proved he was the owner of the car, the police told him that they often

143

found keys in cars, occasionally even in car doors as people rushed to catch trains, but this was the first time they had found the keys in the ignition and the engine still running.

There were two secretaries in the Al Khobar office, both male of course. One, Basheer, was extremely good; the second, Sunderason, was absolutely hopeless. After Glenn Camp had been in the office a couple of months and was making weekly trips to Riyadh, he called back to the office and had the following conversation with Sunderason:

Phone rings.

SUNDERASON: 'Benson & Hedges.'

CAMP: ' "Benson & Hedges?" Who is this?'

SUNDERASON: 'Hi, sir, it's Sunderason, sir.'

CAMP: 'What's the name of our firm?'

SUNDERASON: 'Oh, Benson & Hedges, sir.'

CAMP: 'You had better look for work.'

SUNDERASON: 'Sir, what do you mean?'

CAMP: 'We'll discuss this later.'

He fired him.

One of J&H's contacts in Saudi came on a business trip to New York, where he was put up in the J&H corporate apartment. When John Swarbrick went up-town to meet him, he was greeted by a scene of total devastation. There had obviously been a hell of a party the night before – bodies everywhere, and a considerable number of spare women wandering about. Swarbrick hurriedly alerted Seward, who called Margaret Seebeck, Bob Hatcher's secretary.

SEWARD: 'Margaret, we've had a problem at the apartment. Are you broad-minded?'

MRS SEEBECK: 'Well, I like to think that I am.'

SEWARD: 'I think we've had an orgy there.'

MRS SEEBECK: 'I'm not *that* broad minded.'

On his subsequent visits to New York, that particular contact always found the apartment had been reserved by someone else.

The longest-running saga of all time was getting the licence for J&H to open in Korea. Business in Korea was originally handled from Japan, but in 1980, J&H appointed Tong Jin &

Co. as non-exclusive correspondents to provide local service. It was never intended that they should become the UNISON partner for Korea, but merely be a stop-gap while J&H went through the laborious process of getting their own licence. No one envisaged how long it was going to take, and in 1990 an exasperated Charlie Binford, the country manager in Japan, faxed Martin Rayner in New York to say that he 'would expect to be operational by 1 July 1991. That will only be a short six years, one month, sixteen days and twenty-two hours since you and I sat in front of Lee In Won* and asked for an application form to start this process. P.S. I was hassled by immigration authorities for not having entry stamp in passport as I left Korea. It was there and took them ten minutes to find it. Seemed more than coincidental given events – it's not easy out here in the field.'

If it hadn't been for a stroke of luck, Binford would have retired before J&H ever got their Korean licence. When the Rainoffs lived in Tokyo, among their many bridge partners were the Greggs. By 1990, Don Gregg was the US Ambassador in Korea, and when he saw his old friend's name on the visitors' list for the day, he stopped by to say hello to George. On learning J&H's predicament, he promised to see what he could do. Two months later the licence came through: the Ministry of Finance owed the US a favour.

Charlie Binford thought his career with J&H would end prematurely when Bob Hatcher made a trip to Korea with Martin Rayner just before he retired. Having served in Intelligence during the Korean War, Hatcher was keen to go up to the Demilitarised Zone. The journey coincided with something verging on a monsoon, and when the transport arrived, it turned out to be a forty-seater bus, just for the three of them. They set off in atrocious conditions in the only way the Koreans know how to drive – at break-neck speed – and had almost reached their destination when, failing to stop at a Stop sign, they were rammed amidships by a car, just below where Hatcher was sitting. The death announcement in the *New York Times* flashed before Binford's eyes, but fortunately no one was hurt.

* Director of the Non-Life Insurance Department of the Ministry of Finance.

Both J&H and Willis had interests in Australia. In 1958 J&H appointed the prominent Australian broker Baillieu Insurances Pty, Ltd, as their correspondents, and in 1961 Willis bought an eighty per cent interest in the Sydney-based broker H. B. Nickolls to set up Willis Faber & Nickolls. In 1966 Willis were appointed brokers to Rio Tinto Zinc, whose large Australian subsidiary, Conzinc Rio Tinto of Australia (CRA), used Baillieu. In 1967, eager to expand still further, Willis went on to buy Blick Purdy in Wellington, New Zealand, to act as a subsidiary of Willis Faber & Nickolls. Clearly it would make a lot of sense if Willis and J&H were to join forces and buy Everard Baillieu's family company to retain the important Baillieu name.

Beginning in the autumn of 1968, Dorrance Sexton and David Palmer took it in turns to negotiate with Everard Baillieu on their respective trips to Australia. Baillieu was an unusual character, and dealing with him proved difficult. Even a series of meetings with Sexton and John Roscoe in the Dorchester Hotel in London in July 1969 didn't produce any progress. Then, after six months' silence, Baillieu suggested meeting in Hawaii in early 1970. Roscoe didn't fly,* so Palmer attended for Willis. Baillieu suggested selling a twenty per cent stake in his firm, hedged round with numerous caveats regarding name, control, etc. Whereas Willis might have been prepared to negotiate, Sexton was having none of it, and proposed that Willis and J&H should go it alone and set up a joint company. This they did on 1 July 1970, a fifty-fifty joint venture with Willis having management control. Everard Baillieu behaved impeccably, and transferred all the J&H clients.

It didn't matter whether Willis Faber Johnson & Higgins was managed by Willis, or J&H, or the management was shared – it was never the brightest star in the UNISON network. Nor, with successive socialist governments, was Australia the easiest country in which to be involved in the insurance business – and unlike the UK or the USA, the brightest people didn't choose a career in insurance broking.

When Jan Chelmsford and Colin Methven from Willis were making their first visit to Australia, Colin mentioned on arrival
* He was an aviation broker, and knew much too much about the business.

that he had had a hard time getting his visa. Jan seemed a little surprised, because he didn't have a visa, and he was duly taken off to a separate room at Immigration. Meeting up again at the baggage claim, Chelmsford proudly announced that peers of the realm didn't need visas for Australia.

The non-executive chairman of Willis Faber Johnson & Higgins was Peter Cary, an accountant, who had a large sheep ranch. David Palmer happened to mention on one of his visits that he raised sheep at his country home at Henley-on-Thames. 'How many do you have?' asked Carey. 'Oh, about a hundred,' said Palmer proudly. 'How nice,' replied Carey, who had many thousand. 'Do you know them all by name?' When Dick Purnell took over from Dorrance Sexton, the Purnells and the Palmers had many happy times together Down Under. On arriving in Christchurch, New Zealand, the party was met by a somewhat bemused branch manager in his modest saloon car, to be confronted by four passengers and some twenty items of luggage, most of which belonged to Maggie Purnell. With the help of supporting taxis the party was soon in the Camelot theme hotel, where the Purnells were installed in King Arthur's suite. The bed was completely round and covered in sheepskin. On another trip they all met up for twenty-four hours in Bali before launching into the rigours of a tour of Australia. Dick had purchased a bottle of Champagne on a shopping trip to Denpasar and this was opened with great ceremony before dinner as a treat for the wives. There was an ominous lack of pop – it was Balinese rice wine. Of such experiences are friendships made.

16 The Golden Years

Every great phenomenon, from the Roman Empire to the Welsh Rugby team, has had its golden age, and UNISON was no exception. Its coincided with the reign of Bob Hatcher, the last great chairman of J&H. Robert Vance Hatcher, Jr, was a native of Richmond, Virginia. After Hampden-Sydney College he went on to get a BA in economics from the University of Virginia, 'the University' to everyone in Virginia. After serving in Counter-Intelligence in the Korean War, in 1959 he joined Baker-Cockrell, a small Richmond-based insurance agency owned by friends of

Bob Hatcher

El GRAN BOB!
(Madrid 1983)
BARCA.

his father. This was bought by J&H in 1968, in order to open up in Virginia. The other two partners retired, and Hatcher found himself president of J&H of Virginia. His fellow employees were his secretary, Joan Charles, and E. Massie Valentine, who was eventually to succeed him in Richmond.

Hatcher had charm, connections, drive, and a great sense of humour, but above all he knew how to sell. J&H was soon the leading insurance broker in Virginia, and Hatcher was rewarded by being elected to the board of J&H in 1975. Two years later Dick Purnell made a trip to the Richmond office, and Hatcher arranged to take him to see the Philip Morris plant, a major client of the office. After dinner the night before, Purnell suddenly announced that he was going back to New York in the morning, and asked Bob what he was doing. 'Going to work,' came the reply. 'No you're not,' said Purnell, 'you're going to New York. I want you up there.' 'I'm not sure I want to be in New York,' said Hatcher, who was very much part of the Richmond scene. 'God damn it, I'm offering you the presidency of the company,' snapped Purnell. 'Are you quite sure you know what you're doing?' came the reply.

Hatcher uprooted his family and moved with his wife, Martha Anne, to Greenwich, Connecticut. He brought not only a Southern charm to the executive office, but also a much-needed outsider's perspective. He became the first chairman who had not spent his entire working career at J&H, and the first non-marine man.

By 1977, Purnell had tired of entertaining people from Europe, so Hatcher was given executive responsibility for the European relationships, which by then were of major importance to the firm. The next visitors to New York were Harald Hübener and Christian Dahms, together with their wives, and Bob Hatcher booked a fancy French restaurant for dinner. When the *Maitre D* came round, the Germans went straight ahead and ordered from the menu without requesting the obligatory translation. 'You mean you understand all this stuff?' said Martha Anne. She brought a breath of fresh air to the international entertaining which stood Hatcher in good stead. He made it his business to get to know all the key members of the network, and soon earned their trust and respect. He became particularly close to the Spanish, and great friends with Santi Gil de Biedma.

The boom years of the 1970s and 1980s were years of travel and every multinational risk manager made it his business to go to see his key overseas subsidiaries, accompanied by his UNISON account manager. The clients never failed to be impressed by the quality and responsiveness of their overseas account executives, and how they all appeared to be good friends. This was no act that was put on for the benefit of the client – it would have been impossible to create such a thing. There was a genuine feeling of all being part of some large professional family, and over the years many of the clients felt part of it too.

Behind the scenes, a large investment in time and money was made in sending European account executives to New York and some of the larger J&H branches, and as the network grew, this was extended worldwide. The responsibility for arranging itineraries for these visitors fell on Cathy Monahan, who was assistant to Rudi Portaria and the other area specialists. Cathy was an extremely bright lady, tall, with bedroom eyes and a good sense of humour, who joined J&H in April 1980. When Fernando Gortazar from Gil y Carvajal was visiting New York,

Cathy arranged his itinerary. Now, although Fernando had good English he sometimes had difficulty with the various New York accents, so when Cathy asked him whether he would like to have dinner with her and Hugh Hausman, he heard '. . . and my husband'. Fernando was under the impression that Cathy was still single, but nevertheless accepted the gracious invitation.

At the allotted hour, Fernando went up to her apartment as arranged. He was a little surprised to find Cathy alone and no sign of her husband, but being discreet, did not enquire. When the doorbell rang, Cathy said, 'Ah, here he is,' and in came

Fernando Gortazar

B.
Sept/89

Hugh Hausman. The three of them went out to dinner, and all the time Fernando was thinking how strange it was that these two were married – they were hardly a match, he thought – and how odd that Hugh didn't have a front-door key. Fernando was even more mystified when, once the dinner was over, Hugh offered to take him out to see some night life. 'Oh, do go with him,' whispered Cathy, 'he's been working terribly hard and needs another drink.' It was a very concerned Fernando who came to the office the next morning, only to find that his impressions of Cathy's domestic arrangements were incorrect.

Cathy had been working for the area specialists for a couple of years when Peter Bickett said to George Rainoff one day, 'She's overqualified and overpaid for what she does. Find her something else to do.' George suggested that she become an account executive. 'But we don't have any female account executives,' said Bickett. Rainoff replied, 'That's OK, if she doesn't make it, you can fire her.' She made it.

Raymundo Riestra from Gil y Carvajal was on his first-ever trip to New York, and Cathy scheduled him to have dinner with Hugh Hausman on the Monday night. Hugh was always prepared to give time to the young international visitors, but they had to be prepared to go and have several martinis at the Yale Club before heading on to dinner. Raymundo, still suffering from jet-lag, was not familiar with the strength of the New York cocktails, and once in the restaurant, got up from the table to go to the men's room and promptly passed out. Hugh, who hadn't noticed, was still explaining the finer points of the J&H manuscript form. Ever after Riestra was known throughout UNISON as Raymundo Siesta.

Although they all had their individual foibles, the majority of risk managers were grateful for the help provided by the UNISON offices when they travelled, but there were exceptions. Some American risk managers regarded their trips to Europe as an important perk of the job and were determined to have as good a time as possible without ever putting their hands in their corporate pockets. On one such occasion, a risk manager visiting Gras Savoye in Paris ordered *haricots verts aux truffes* as his appetiser for dinner, quite obviously the most expensive thing on the menu. When it arrived, he solemnly scraped all the black stuff off his green beans before eating them, much to the amazement of the waiters.

Risk managers visiting London invariably asked to be taken to the latest show. At one point Ian Macalpine-Leny had to impose a rule that he wouldn't go and see *Starlight Express* more than once a week, whoever the client. Others expected to take advantage of their wives being left at home to do things that they normally only did in their dreams.

In addition to being responsible for the 'reverse flow' business coming back into the US, Rudi Portaria performed the key function of leading the international account executive training courses in Europe twice a year. These had the dual purpose of raising the professional standard of the participants, and getting them to know each other. When the meetings were hosted by Gras Savoye in Paris, everyone stayed at the Meridien Hotel at Porte Maillot, a well known spot for extra-curricular activities. The ladies in question used to follow guests up in the elevator and offer their services, having first discovered their nationality. Flavio Amoroso presented them with a problem. Although Italian he had been born and raised in South Africa, and with his RAF handle-bar moustache and braces (suspenders), he would have passed for a Brit anywhere. Taking no chances, the lady in question knocked on his door and asked *'Compagnie?'*, to which Flavio answered, 'Johnson & Higgins.'

On another occasion a participant from Willis's company in Dublin, on his first-ever trip to the USA, excused himself during the morning coffee break of the meeting in St Louis, and went across the street to a bank to change some travellers' cheques; he returned at four o'clock. He had been caught up in a bank robbery and detained as a hostage.

When European clients travelled to see their US subsidiaries, it was the foreign reps who were there to oil the wheels and ensure that J&H in their turn provided seamless service. There was none better than Jack Birtwhistle, the company secretary of Hepworth Ceramic Holdings, who travelled over every year with his Willis account director from the Sheffield office, Peter Ledger. The US account was co-ordinated in St Louis, but visits had to be made to plants involving other J&H offices. This included Seattle, when Jack famously remarked of Denver Ginsey, the director in charge of the office, 'I don't know what effect he has on his staff, but he scared the hell out of me.' Hepworth was a huge client for the St Louis office, and J&H did a first-rate job. In addition to a lot of hard work, there was always a barbecue at the branch manager's house, and a trip to watch the Cardinals.* Jack Birtwhistle was an astute, demanding but appreciative client, and very good company to travel with – apart from the fact that he never wanted to go to bed.

One year the familiar handle-bar moustache of Humphrey Crook, the J&H account manager, was missing – Mrs Crook had evidently got tired of it – and nothing seemed quite the same. The problem was solved by Ian Macalpine-Leny, who spotted a theatrical costume shop on the way back to the hotel. A replacement was bought, Humphrey was blindfolded at the end of the final meeting, and with the help of some theatrical glue, he was sent home to Mrs Crook looking much like his former self. Such things are good for client relationships.

When Willis won the BTR account, Bob Cameron was very worried that the US business would be co-ordinated out of New York and the Boston office would lose Stowe Woodward, the subsidiary they already held as a client. Calling the account manager, Heidi Scheller, into his office, he asked what they could arrange which would be fun enough to entice the BTR insurance manager to Boston on his forthcoming trip. 'Gee, why don't we take him sailing?' said Heidi. 'Sailing?' replied Cameron. 'You have a sailboat? A big sailboat?' 'Sure,' said Heidi, 'thirty-four foot, and easily large enough to take everyone.' 'I must be paying you too much,' said Cameron, reaching for the phone to call the Willis account director, Bob Guthrie.

A day sailing off Boston sounded much more appealing to Mike Porter than one watching golf in New York, so after the meetings in New York, Mike, Bob and Ian Macalpine-Leny flew up to Boston. The following day they were driven down to the dock at Scituate by the delightful Boston marine manager, Bill Hutchins, who proceeded to unload crates of Samuel Adams

* The St Louis baseball team.

and carrier bags stuffed with Cape Cod potato chips, fresh bread and pastrami, on to the dock. Heidi had invited her brother and his fiancée to come and help crew the boat, and a very attractive American Airlines hostess, Pam Coffin, to make up numbers.

It was a glorious day with plenty of wind, and the Sam Adams and Cape Cod chips went down a treat. Bob Guthrie photographed both the boat and Pam in her bikini from every conceivable angle. At the end of the day, 'Hutch' literally poured the three Brits onto the plane back to London, and everyone was asleep, still clutching what was left of the Cape Cod chips, before the plane was pushed back from the gate. Back in London some time later, Mrs Guthrie opened Bob's photographs that had arrived through the post, and immediately suffered a sense of humour failure. No matter; there was no question in Mike Porter's mind – his account was going to be serviced out of Boston.

The real strength of UNISON was its ability to service global insurance programmes by providing first-rate service anywhere in the world controlled from one UNISON office. Here sat the account director who dealt direct with the client, and was responsible for the entire account worldwide. This was achieved by strict adherence to a code of practice. An incident involving Peter Ledger, soon after he took over responsibility for all the incoming J&H business to Willis's Sheffield office, illustrates how effective this was in practice. One of his first meetings was with Keith White, the group risk manager of Cummins Engine, who was over from Indiana. At the end of the meeting, White issued a string of instructions for Peter to implement. This was fine, except Peter was acutely aware that taking direct instructions from the client without the knowledge of the J&H account manager in the US would result in a fate worse than death. With some trepidation, Peter mumbled something about also having to tell J&H.

He knew that something was wrong when this was met with bemused silence, and a look of consternation on the face of the Willis account director. White's silence hung over the three of them like the eerie lull before a thunderstorm. Then it broke.

'Who the hell are J&H?' Peter's predecessor had failed to tell him that Cummins was a direct Willis Faber appointment, and nothing to do with J&H.*

Whenever UNISON people were gathered together, every opportunity was taken to involve clients and prospective clients. At one such memorable occasion in Stockholm the keynote speaker began his presentation: 'Clients of UNISON, prospective clients of UNISON, and hopeless friends.' No one took this concept further than Lucho Paz Soldan, who hosted the first regional conference for Latin American property loss control engineers (fire surveyors) in Lima when he was country manager for Peru. Every evening after the meetings for the ten engineers had finished, there was an 'event'. The first night there was a dinner hosted by the AIU at a restaurant where every dish was based on potatoes, after which at least a third of the attendees got sick; the second night was a dinner at the Jockey Club, the most prestigious men's club in Lima; the third night was the big bash, to which Lucho invited his most important clients, prospective clients, and all the prominent people in Lima, together with their wives. The party was held round the pool at La Granja Azul resort accompanied by a twenty-five-piece orchestra. The main event was a display of folk dancing by the National Peruvian Ballet Company, followed by dancing into the small hours. As the ten engineers didn't have anyone to dance with they watched the ballet and went to bed. The final day included a sightseeing trip followed by a dinner at the famous chicken restaurant at La Granja Azul. Normal convention for such conferences was that the cost was split between the offices of the participants, but Lucho had a few problems when he tried to charge out his costs for these three days.

Encouraged by the success of the UNISON network and the genuine pleasure of working with network people, friendships sprang up at every level. It wasn't at all unusual for many international people to feel that they had more in common with their UNISON colleagues than they had with those in their own firm. They became mutual godparents, arranged international exchanges for their children and, tired of the endless UNISON

* 'Peter's predecessor' was hardly to blame – he had just been fired.

155

golf days, Javier Barcaiztegui even arranged a UNISON partridge shoot.

On the business level, exchanges were given a further boost by the instigation of the Ken Childs Scholarship, in memory of the Willis deputy chairman who died prematurely in 1984. Childs was head of Willis's wholesaling side so was never involved with UNISON, but he was always the greatest supporter of J&H. The objective was to increase the links between Willis and J&H by sending one bright young Willis person to J&H and an equally bright young J&H-er to Willis for training every year. The first recipient from J&H in 1985 was Mary Claiborne, the future Mrs Frediani.

Hugh Hausman and David Frediani set off from 95 Wall Street one evening on what was a well-worn path for Hugh: cocktails at the bar in the old J. P. Morgan apartment at the top of Wall Street, then up on the Lexington Line to Grand Central

David Frediani

Station and more drinks and dinner at the Yale Club. By the time they got out at Grand Central Station it was snowing heavily. Some time later, after a good dinner, there was a complete white-out, and the whole city had come to an absolute standstill. There were several feet of snow and nothing on the street except a large stretch limo, parked – as Manhattan limos always are – with its engine running, right outside the Yale Club. Hugh went up to the car and tapped on the window, and the driver rolled it down. 'Ah, any chance of giving us a ride up-town.' 'I'm terribly sorry,' came back the reply, 'but I'm already taken.' 'It's a dreadful night,' said Hugh, 'would you mind if we ask whoever has hired you if we may share a ride uptown?' 'Not at all,' said the driver, 'it's Mr Lovejoy.'

Hugh disappeared back into the Yale Club and asked for Mr Lovejoy at the desk, obtained his room number, and called up the room. 'I'm really sorry to disturb you,' began Hugh, 'but I'm Hugh Hausman – you won't know me but I need to get up-town fairly urgently and as there's a really bad snow condition outside, I was wondering if I could share your limo.' 'No problem,' answered Mr Lovejoy, 'I'll come down and speak to the driver.' Five minutes went by, ten, then after fifteen minutes Hugh went to the phone again. 'I'm really sorry to disturb you again Mr Lovejoy, but I do really need to get up-town.' 'So sorry, I'll be right down,' came the reply.

Five minutes later the elevator doors opened and out stepped this dashing fellow with his hair slicked back, obviously straight out of the shower, with a very attractive young lady, also straight out of the shower. Hugh introduced himself, they climbed in and set off very slowly. They were the only vehicle on Park Avenue and people were beginning to appear on skis. Hugh, pretty incoherent by this time, started to tell Mr Lovejoy about J&H and UNISON. He and his companion looked at each other but, wanting to be polite, offered Hugh a drink. There was no ice, so Mr Lovejoy rolled down a window and took some snow off the top of the car. Hugh was still in mid flow about the wonders of UNISON. Gradually they inched their way up town and finally arrived outside Hugh's building. Mr Lovejoy offered to take David Frediani on, but David thought it was better to see Hugh safely inside. A snow-plough had been through, and there was a huge pile of snow outside the building. Overcoat on, hat pushed on the back of his head and still clutching his briefcase, Hugh staggered up the huge mound of snow, only to fall headfirst into the snowdrift with just his legs sticking out and his briefcase off to the side. By this time the doorman had come out to help Frediani drag Hugh out, and get him inside.

A few days later Hugh received a call from the Yale Club about a bill that they were not sure how to deal with. The bill for the limo had not been paid, nor had the enormous Club bill for Champagne, drinks and dinners run up by Mr Lovejoy. The problem was that he was a reciprocal member and they had no means of tracing him. As they knew Hugh was a friend of his, they wondered if he could help. Hugh quickly explained that he had only asked him for a ride up-town, and had never met him before in his life. Mr Lovejoy turned out to be an impostor.

As time and excess inevitably took their toll, Hugh began to slow up. The offices in 125 Broad Street were fitted with motion sensors to ensure that the lights went off when they weren't occupied. Hugh frequently found himself sitting in the dark in the afternoon. He was eventually pushed out of J&H in 1991, and was last heard of travelling to Uzbekistan with a group of executives to advise on insurance company investments. He retired to Seattle, and died following a heart attack on the operating table in 2001.

All this time the UNISON network was continuing to expand, and partners were added throughout Scandinavia and Eastern Europe. By the end of the 1980s, UNISON could boast some 13,000 employees in 191 offices, in 56 countries. Flushed with the success of the newly launched brand, Christian Dahms introduced the San Francisco-based image consultants, Landor Associates, who were invited to put together a proposal for marketing the UNISON brand. Significantly, after a preliminary presentation, they declined to accept the proposal, telling the PWG that UNISON wasn't yet ready to take this step.

For all the outward success there were some fundamental problems, which increasingly dominated all internal meetings.

There was only exclusivity between J&H and the European partners, several of whom had subsidiaries in other partners' countries; there was no financial commitment between the partners, and UNISON had no strategic plan and therefore no co-ordinated direction. There was also concern that the liberalisation anticipated from the introduction of Freedom of Services in Europe in 1992 would further erode UNISON's competitive advantage. An early proposal was to have an exchange of shareholdings between the major partners. A fervent believer in this concept and always one to take decisive action when he believed it was correct, Santi Gil stunned the 1985 conference in Marbella by offering twenty-five per cent of Gil y Carvajal to J&H, and a further twenty-five per cent to be split between Willis and Jauch & Hübener. Christian Dahms strongly supported this but was unable to convince his fellow partners. Willis thought the price was too high and dithered. J&H went ahead with their twenty-five per cent in 1989, which they subsequently increased to fifty per cent.

J&H and Willis had meanwhile entered a round of discussions in 1985 to try and find some workable formula to join the two companies together – they had, after all, worked together for almost one hundred years. Every conceivable mechanism employed by other organisations was considered, the meetings consumed more and more time and energy, but failed to make any progress. Meanwhile another initiative had got off the ground – to form a holding company based in Brussels. There wasn't any clear idea exactly what UNISON SA would do, but it had its first officers: Ken Seward was elected president at the Rome conference in 1987, and Dany Kervyn, for legal reasons, *administrateur délégué.**

A steering committee was set up consisting of Ken Seward, Adrian Gregory, Christian Dahms and Patrick Lucas, with Dany Kervyn representing the smaller UNISON partners and acting as secretary. It was decided to open an office in Brussels to act as a flagship European office for UNISON, and be involved in co-ordinating cross-border business. Arthur Andersen were engaged in early 1989 to come up with a strategic review, curi-

* Managing director.

ously referred to as the 'Stockholm Protocol', which would include alternative structures and a recommended solution. Unfortunately it was discovered that their recommended approach was in contravention of European Community competition rules, and they sheepishly returned their fee. In spite of this, the steering committee agreed to press on with opening the Brussels office, and the search began for a general manager.

The most outstanding candidate was Jerry Karter, who was manager of the international department in New York. A Dutchman who had spent most of his working life in Europe, he joined J&H in New York from the INA (Insurance Company of North America), and quickly worked his way up to become the manager. An impressive-looking man with a penchant for Cuban cigars, he would carry just the weight needed for the job. Like all workaholics, Jerry Karter always got to the office between 7 and 7.30 a.m. Unlocking his office door one morning, there inside the door he saw a huge computer print-out reading 'Happy Fiftieth Birthday, Jerry.' Before he could react, the entire international department crowded into his office and sang 'Happy Birthday'. Out from the crowd stepped Karl DeFoe clutching a beautifully tied package. 'Jerry,' he said, 'a fiftieth birthday is a very special occasion, and so we've all put some money together to buy you something really fantastic.' Quite overcome by this time, Jerry unwrapped a box of his favourite Cuban cigars. He couldn't believe his eyes: Karl DeFoe was the most vehement anti-smoker in the office, and had long waged war on Jerry and his cigars. 'On second thoughts,' said Karl taking the box back from Jerry, 'I don't think this is a very good idea', and he proceeded to put it on the floor and jump on it. Karter was completely speechless. His life had just ended. Only then did he notice that the box was empty. Grudgingly, New York agreed to release Jerry, and he initially accepted the Brussels assignment. But about that time he also received an offer from SCOR to head up their US reinsurance company. Knowing that his wife didn't want to go back to Europe, and after a huge amount of heart-searching, he eventually withdrew and went to SCOR.

With Jerry Karter out of the frame, Willis proposed Nick Davenport. Although as far as Christian Dahms was concerned he was 'just another bloody wholesaler', Nick was an inspired choice. He was brought up in Latin America and spoke Spanish as a child, had fluent French and passable German. After joining Willis in 1971, he was sent out after barely two years to open the very successful Willis Faber Boels & Bégault joint reinsurance company in Brussels. In 1976 he had the much more difficult job of starting Gras Savoye Willis Faber in Paris, because Patrick Lucas was a very different kettle of fish from Lucien Bégault. Arriving back in London in 1980 with a French wife, he headed up the team dealing with reinsurance in French-speaking Africa and, for some obscure reason, Greece.

In 1987, Willis sent Nick on the three month executive programme at INSEAD, based in Fontainebleau. INSEAD insisted that alumni should nominate a project based on what they had learned to apply to their own companies on their return. Nick chose '1992' (the introduction of Freedom of Services in the EC), a subject that at the time was completely unknown in Willis. Despite his paper arriving on David Palmer's desk on the day that the acquisition of Stewart Wrightson was announced, the board liked it, and Lord Chelmsford was asked at the end of 1987 to set up a strategy group chaired by Ian Macalpine-Leny, with Nick as deputy. Now, Ian didn't know anything about 1992 either, but took a great liking to Nick, was keen to learn, and readily proposed that they should put titles aside and just do a first-class job. It didn't take Nick long to see the merits of Ian's UNISON approach, and he soon put aside his wholesaling bias and became a convert, helped by seeing UNISON in action in visits to Jauch & Hübener and Gil y Carvajal. So when Adrian Gregory approached him later in the year about the UNISON job, Nick was very interested.

Behind Adrian Gregory's vague and eccentric exterior, there was an acute brain and a gift for bringing opposing parties together, and he soon got the agreement of the steering committee. Nick then set out on a one-month familiarisation programme in J&H New York that was to take him to every part of the organisation. Knowing his susceptibility to attractive and intelligent women, Ian arranged for both of them to have dinner with Margo Bowden of J&H corporate communications on his first night in New York. After that, the success of the visit was assured. Nick was seduced by the sheer class and professionalism of J&H. Those who had invented the art taught him the international retail business. As for UNISON, there was never a problem – Nick was already committed.

In addition to being extremely bright and very much a true European, Nick Davenport was a gifted speaker. He gave the keynote address on '1992' at the 1989 RIMS conference in Monte Carlo, which did much to raise the profile of UNISON SA. He then set about finding office space in Brussels, hiring a secretary, and making arrangements to move his family out at the end of the school year. But Nick was to locate and furnish offices in the Square de Meeûs in Brussels that he would never occupy, and to hire an attractive secretary to whom he would never dictate a letter. There were moves afoot known only to the main board of Willis which would bring the golden age abruptly to a close.

Tom Pappas

17 Decline . . .

It didn't need a rocket scientist to realise the incredible potential that a merger between J&H and Willis would create. Willis was supreme in reinsurance and wholesaling; J&H was a first-class retail broker built on total dedication to client service. Culturally the two firms were very similar, and had a history of working together for over ninety years. By the middle of the 1980s, J&H and Willis between them produced the lion's share of business coming into the UNISON network, and Willis was J&H's principal access to the London market. A merger between these two blue chip brokers would see UNISON's position as the leading servicing network for multinational companies become unassailable. Also, although the informal arrangement between Willis and J&H had served both firms well for so long, Willis, now a major public company, needed a permanent arrangement to secure access to the all-important North American market. Again, the obvious solution was to find a way of merging the two firms.

We have already seen that a merger was first suggested as early as 1898, and further attempts were made periodically over the years. There must have been a strong possibility that if Derek Ripley had lived, he and Dorrance Sexton would have carried off the golden prize. The task became immensely more difficult after Willis became a public company in 1976, quite apart from the differing priorities and personalities of successive chairmen. Sexton and Roscoe were not good chemistry, nor were Purnell and Taylor. With Hatcher and Palmer there were once again two men who made it their top priority to bring the two firms together. J&H acquired five per cent of Willis in 1985 in what seemed to some a natural prelude to a full-scale bid.*

* On a visit to Willis's Sheffield office, Palmer was asked about this share deal. He was very open and said that Hatcher had approached him and asked if the Willis board would support J&H acquiring 25% of the shares. This would have shut out any other bidders. Palmer told him that as Willis was a public company, J&H would either have to make a full bid or limit themselves to no more than 5%.

But it never came. Instead there was increasing grit in the works. Willis acquired a major stake in Global Special Risks in New Orleans, as a source of US oil & gas business* in 1984, and then in 1987 bought Stewart Wrightson, a large predominantly domestic UK broker. Not only did Willis want to strengthen the retail side of their business, which lagged a long way behind wholesale and reinsurance in contribution to group profits, but David Palmer wanted to acquire David Rowland, Stewart Wrightson's very able chairman, as his successor.† Stewart Wrightson owned Stewart Smith, a US surplus lines broker,‡ and, partly in retaliation, J&H acquired Carter Brito e Cunha in 1988 to form J&H Ltd, a wholesale and reinsurance broker at Lloyd's. To many of the old Willis hands this was the writing on the wall.§

The merger discussions that had been instigated in 1985 by David Palmer but never made any real progress were started up again by Roger Elliott when he took over as chairman of Willis at the end of 1988. Richard Dalzell had joined from Trafalgar House as finance director designate in April 1989, and on 1 July joined the board in that role to replace John Robins, who moved on to special projects. The Willis team then became Elliott, Gregory, Robins and Dalzell.

There were always going to be problems in coming up with a structure that would put together a public and a private company, quite apart from continuing to pay retiring J&H directors for ten years after they had left the board, but the discussions never got as far as that. The principal stumbling block was who would control Willis Wrightson, Willis's UK retail company, with Willis refusing to agree to control passing to J&H. In consequence, J&H were not prepared to give up control of J&H Ltd,

* J&H were not strong in the oil and gas business, nor were Willis.
† When the time came, the Willis board wouldn't accept him. Roger Elliott was appointed chairman, and David Rowland left to become chairman of Sedgwick. He went on to become chairman of Lloyd's.
‡ Authorised to place business with insurers outside its own State.
§ There was concern on the J&H board that Willis, as a public company, might be acquired by a US competitor in an unfriendly takeover, thus disrupting J&H's access to the London market. The Carter Brito acquisition was regarded as a hedge against that possibility.

their Lloyd's broker in London. It became apparent that the J&H team wanted control over any merged company, although J&H was smaller than Willis and less profitable.

The discussions staggered on, but there were serious doubters on both sides. Bob Hatcher was determined to do a deal, but he didn't realise until too late that the team he put in charge of the negotiations had no intention of doing so. By the end of 1989, Willis had given up hope of ever doing anything with J&H. J&H Ltd had caused major unease in London, and it was perceived that the threat of transferring all wholesale business to J&H Ltd would be used to force the price of Willis below that which the shareholders would be prepared to accept. And yet Willis had to have earnings on the ground in America, without which they could never expect to remain in the first division. Adrian Gregory, now deputy chairman and ever the great politician on the Willis board, had been saying for some time that Willis must have a 'plan B'. The board decided to accept his advice, and Booz Allen were commissioned to prepare a report on US brokers.

Once Marsh & McLennan, Alexander & Alexander and J&H had been discounted, top of the list was Corroon & Black, a broker specialising in 'middle market' business where there was no risk manager or insurance department. To many, it was inconceivable that Willis could ever do a deal with a second-division US broker like Corroon & Black, but that was to underestimate the influence and personality of Bob Corroon, the chairman. Bob Corroon could well have been a director of J&H, and Willis immediately felt comfortable with him.

In the spring of 1989 Jennifer Cartmell, treasurer and chief development officer of Corroon & Black, was on a panel at a Russell Miller* symposium where the keynote speaker was the recently retired David Palmer. During a cocktail reception that evening, David approached her, and said, after listening to her comments, 'We should talk.' Jennifer told him that her firm would 'love to talk, but you are already married.' David gave her that wonderful smile of his and repeated, 'We should talk.' Cartmell relayed this conversation back to Bob Corroon, who

* Boutique mergers and acquisitions consulting firm based in San Francisco.

after some initial scepticism decided to call Roger Elliott. Elliott met him in his suite at the Hyde Park Hotel in London, and it soon became apparent that a deal could be done. Corroon's two stipulations were that 'Corroon' should be in the name of the merged company, and that the Corroon & Black CEO, Dick Miller, should be CEO. On the face of it this would be a perfect match with virtually no areas of overlap. Not until too late was it discovered that the due diligence exercise had not included a box labelled 'culture'. Negotiations went on apace, the boards first met on Presidents' Day, 19 February 1990, and in three weeks there was an agreement in principle. The respective teams then got down to work in earnest in an atmosphere of the utmost secrecy.

Once the due diligence had got under way, Richard Dalzell began to have serious misgivings about some of the findings, not least of which was the enormous head office building that Corroon & Black had commissioned in Nashville, Tennessee. He suggested that Willis should have a fall-back position in the event that the deal became too unsatisfactory or too expensive. This was thrown out in no uncertain terms by the merchant bankers, who not surprisingly were firmly focused on completing the deal and collecting their fee.

With the announcement set for Monday 4 June 1990, Roger Elliott, Adrian Gregory and John Robins had to attend the UNI-SON conference in Rotterdam in May, which was held, ominously, on the fiftieth anniversary of the German bombing of the city. It was not a great conference, and the Willis team kept as low a profile as possible, while all the time giving the appearance that everything was normal. Ian Macalpine-Leny attended on a break from his business school in Lausanne, only to discover that the negotiations with J&H had been broken off. Fearing the worst, he e-mailed Nick Davenport on his return to Switzerland: 'In the absence of any further instructions from the bridge, I'll continue to rearrange the chairs on the deck of the *Titanic*.' Nick had been fully aware of what was going on for some time, and couldn't say a word.

At the end of May, J&H held their board meeting in London. The climax of the week's events was a black-tie dinner on Thursday 24 May hosted by Willis at the Imperial War Museum. One or two of the J&H directors sensed something was wrong, but no one could put a finger on it. Ken Hecken, considered by the Willis team to be the most intransigent of the J&H negotiating directors, was placed under the V-2 rocket.*

On Saturday 2 June, Bob Hatcher was in Paris, and Roger Elliott flew over to break the news to him, while Adrian Gregory flew to Mülheim to see Christian Dahms.† On Sunday 3 June, all the senior executives of Willis were called together in Ten Trinity Square to be told that at 8 a.m. the following morning, Willis would be informing the London Stock Exchange of the acquisition of Corroon & Black and the formation of Willis Corroon. Ian Macalpine-Leny, who had been due to set off for a week's salmon fishing on the river Helmsdale, drove back south for the meeting. It confirmed his worst fears. Ten years of work had come to nothing. On arriving back in Lincolnshire he briefly described to his wife Anne what had gone on. 'How do you spell "Corroon?"' she asked; then, after a pause, 'What's going to happen to all our friends?' and burst into tears. Jennifer Cartmell had been a key member of the Corroon & Black acquisition team, and was responsible with the chief financial officer for the due diligence exercise. Despite several rumours, there was never any leak, and her husband was CFO of Marsh & McLennan's broking subsidiary . . .

With absolutely no inkling of what was to come, the announcement on Monday 4 June 1990 was like a bombshell. Throughout UNISON there was shock, disbelief and immense sadness, but also a sense of betrayal. On the international retail side of Willis, everyone was completely numb. J&H had been the cornerstone of everything, and the UNISON network had been integral to all major client production initiatives.

J&H had been caught totally unprepared,* and their major task was to replace Willis's servicing capability in the UK as

* The first long-range ballistic missile, used with devastating effect by the Germans on London and the cities of south-east England from the autumn of 1944.
† They called Ken Seward at home to tell him.

soon as possible. Everyone assumed that they would buy a UK retail broker, but each one investigated carried so much baggage that the decision was made in June 1991 to build their own company in the UK. This they did with great speed, creating a credible retail broker in twelve months. Willis on the other hand had to recreate their own UNISON network, which took considerably longer, but under Adrian Gregory's leadership, Nick Davenport and Sarah Turvill soon had the beginnings of a sound network in Europe. In 1994, the members of RIMS voted the Willis Corroon network number one for service.

Willis's problem, however, lay in the US. Corroon & Black turned out to be a hastily assembled franchise with some very good parts, and some not so good. This was exacerbated by complete indecision on the part of the new Willis Corroon board for two and a half years as to how to move forward. Once Corroon & Black had discovered that it would be Roger Elliott as executive chairman and not Dick Miller as CEO who would run the new company, their job descriptions were fudged so as to be almost identical. This ran on down through the senior management structure, and was in part responsible for the subsequent procrastination, almost invariably fatal with any take-over or merger with a US company. Given a dead-end with J&H, a merger with another US broker was the right thing to do, but Willis had the wrong expectation as to the outcome, and the wrong management structure to make it work. The end result was to put Willis back more than ten years in the US. In spite of this, Willis was to emerge as the third-largest global insurance broker, and the only one of the original UNISON partners to remain independent.

When Willis moved to Ten Trinity Square, the directors of J&H presented the main board with a magnificent long-case clock that stood in the board room. The accompanying plaque read: 'This clock was presented by Johnson & Higgins to Willis

* In 1989, disillusioned with being international manager of J&H in Philadelphia, Jim Hutchin was interviewing with Corroon & Black. During one interview, he was left with the distinct impression that Corroon & Black were talking to Willis. On deciding to stay with J&H, he wrote a paper entitled 'Why Willis Faber and Corroon & Black will merge'. No one took any notice.

Faber Ltd on the occasion of their move to Ten Trinity Square and in recognition and appreciation of a friendship and valued relationship that knows no bounds in time. May 1977.' It is still there, but the plaque has long since disappeared.

In business, everything is achievable if it is wanted badly enough. Even the problems of combining a public and a private company could have been overcome if the resolve had been there; but it wasn't. Both sides had been intransigent, and Willis had been too hasty to break with J&H. In the opinion of one member of the Willis team, with so much at stake, both sides should have withdrawn for a couple of months to reconsider, and then tried again with different teams. But others believed that it was the end of the road.

UNISON had been dealt a mortal blow. On the face of it, the edifice remained unchanged, albeit minus one of its principal legs, but underneath the belief in its sustainability as a virtual organisation without ownership had been damaged beyond repair. The gas had started to escape from the balloon, and sooner or later the basket would begin to lose height.

18 Borrowed Time

It took some time to recover from the paralysis brought about by the Willis news. Fortunately, no one wanted to lose any clients, so Willis Corroon was perfectly happy to continue to service UNISON business, and UNISON the old Willis business. Such were the friendships and good-will that existed among the UNISON family that it was very much business as usual as far as the clients were concerned.

By March 1991, J&H had decided to build their own retail company in the UK, and started looking for a CEO. As so often is the case in the insurance business, they found one on the golf course. Patrick Franklin-Adams was on 'gardening leave' from Sedgwick prior to becoming CEO of Heath's UK retail company. With the ingenuity that could only have come from the involvement of a head-hunter, Patrick found himself partnering Nuno de Brito e Cunha, co-chairman of J&H's London-based wholesaling company, at Lloyd's versus Lucifer's at Walton Heath. Twenty-four hours later he was on board. Ironically, his uncle Murrough Turvill had been a main board director of Willis Faber, and he had actually agreed to join Willis to be number two to Adrian Gregory when Adrian was so ill in the early 80s. On offering his resignation to Sedgwick, he was told in no uncertain terms 'You can't join Willis – they don't even own their own network.' So he told David Palmer that he had changed his mind.

Reporting to J&H director Dick Meyer who had transferred to London from New York the previous July to run J&H's UK interests, Franklin-Adams set to work to build up his team. Paul Merlino and Chip Bechtold were seconded from the USA, and five or six account executives were persuaded to join from Willis, but the majority of the new team came from elsewhere in the market. With no one hiring due to the down-turn in the market, J&H were not short of applicants. By the time Meyer returned to New York in January 1992, J&H Ltd and the new retail company, J&H UK Ltd, had more than three hundred and fifty people in the UK. They did a very credible job, but as far as

CHIP, KINDLY *REQUESTING* A U.K RISK MANAGER WHETHER HE PREFERS WILLIS or UNISON...

Chip Bechtold

Sorry, Chip!
B.
LONDON. vac. Jan/92

the rest of UNISON was concerned, it wasn't quite the same.

Paul Merlino owed his selection for London to spending a period training in Willis's international unit in Ipswich in May and June of 1990. Once on board, he quickly began servicing the transferred business. As the European account manager for Gillette, he was asked at short notice in February 1993 to prepare a due diligence report on a new Gillette acquisition in St Petersburg. This involved a trip to the new company along with a senior man from Gillette Europe. When the managing director of Gillette's joint venture partner, Lennits, who made everything from military hardware to religious icons, discovered that Paul's mother was Russian Orthodox, he kindly presented him with a gift of a new icon. Unfortunately, being made of copper and wood it set off the metal detector at the airport, and he was under arrest – you weren't allowed to take icons out of the country. 'But it's new,' protested Paul. 'Take a look.' Unfortunately, the customs manual didn't make any exception for new icons. The Gillette man quickly came over to see what the problem was, followed by the team from Lennits. With Russian voices getting raised in what was rapidly becoming a heated argument, the local managing director told Paul to get on the plane to Gdansk; they would take care of it.

There was no seat assignment, and the first thing he noticed when he got on board was that all the Russians took window seats, so the foreign travellers had to take the aisle seats. And there were no seat belts. As the plane became airborne and started to climb, he had the sensation of falling backwards; the young woman in the seat in front of ended up in his lap, and they both in turn fell backwards on to the old lady sitting behind them. The only way to escape was to roll into the aisle. Then the panelling started falling off, and the stewardesses came calmly down the plane putting it back again. Once they had reached their cruising altitude, it became immediately apparent why the Russians had taken the window seats: so much condensation appeared in the cabin that it literally started to rain, but the window seats were protected by the overhang of the luggage lockers. Elsewhere, the regular travellers took out plastic folders to place over their heads, as this was clearly a normal occurrence. On landing, the managing director from Gillette was really quite upset. 'Doesn't this airline care about safety?' he asked the stewardess. 'Oh yes,' she replied with a lovely smile. 'The safest place is on our international flights – you have to be careful about the domestic flights.'

Two days after the Gillette report had been delivered, Coca-Cola announced they were opening up in Moscow. Patrick Franklin-Adams and John Gussenhoven, who had taken over from Dick Meyer as chairman of J&H Holdings, the parent company of all J&H interests in the UK, called Merlino in and asked him to go and prepare another report, and at the same time investigate the feasibility of opening a J&H office in Moscow. So it was that Paul Merlino, one of the few Japanese-speaking Americans in the whole of J&H, was sent to Russia. This conformed to the unwritten J&H rule that no one was ever sent overseas anywhere they could actually speak the language. Bob Schram left Harvard with a degree in Asian Studies and Economics speaking Malay, Indonesian and Tagalog, so he was sent to Brazil, though he didn't speak a single word of Portuguese; Bill Jones spent a year learning French at Berlitz, married his French teacher, and was promptly sent to Taiwan; similarly, Ken Koff spent eighteen months learning Farsi, and was then sent to China; Jim Hutchin majored in Asian Studies, and spoke Mandarin Chinese, so was sent to Mexico; Joe Dell, who spoke Italian, was sent to Singapore; Svein Tyldrum's Norwegian and Japanese served no obvious purpose in Brazil; Drew Haaser's Portuguese didn't help in Korea; Erik Severeid is said to have spoken Norwegian in Germany, German in France, and French in Washington, DC. Hugh Hausman was at the other extreme: despite spending twenty years overseas, he was completely incapable of learning to speak anything.

The office in Moscow was set up as a joint venture between J&H and Jauch & Hübener. Volker Preuss, one of the partners of Jauch & Hübener, introduced Victor Tarasov from the Ingostrokh, who became the man on the ground, with Paul Merlino spending three out of every four weeks travelling through the countries of the Russian Federation servicing business. Paul was soon to discover that the Russians had a good sense of humour. In a country where general pleasantries were a necessary prelude to any business discussion, it was usual for a new arrival to be asked what were his impressions of the country. Keen to be up-beat about his hosts, Paul would mention the great possibilities, how the people were very intelligent, the wealth of natural resources – also that it seemed to him that everyone had sad stories about the recent past and there was pessimism, despite a great future in prospect.

'I don't see a pessimism,' said the chairman of one of the major insurance companies in Moscow. 'Russia is a very optimistic country. Have you ever seen that famous picture in the Louvre of Adam and Eve in the Garden?' he asked, with a twinkle in his eye. Merlino had to admit he hadn't. 'Well, you should see it,' he said. 'Now I'll tell you a famous Russian story. There

173

was a Frenchman, an Englishman and a Russian in the Louvre looking at that picture, and the Frenchman said, "This picture reminds me of France." "Why is that?" the others asked. "The figure of the woman, the physique of the man – so French." The Englishman said, "This picture reminds me of England." "Why is that?" they asked. "The clear bright water, the beautiful garden – so English." Then the Russian said, "You are both wrong. This picture is of Russia; there's no food, no clothing, and they think they are in Paradise." Russians are very optimistic people.'

Doing business in Russia so soon after the break-up of the Soviet Union was not without its excitements. Earlier on, Merlino had set up a series of visits without the help of Victor Tarasov. Bill Remington, the J&H director in Houston, had given him an introduction to one of the deputy prime ministers, who in turn had set up meetings with members of the City of Moscow Council. The meetings took place, and Merlino gave everyone a J&H information pack and a small gift of a J&H clock.

On arriving back at his hotel, Merlino took a call from someone from an insurance company who wanted to meet with him that evening. Merlino said he was very sorry, he had a dinner with a client that night and was leaving the next morning, but would gladly arrange a meeting on his next visit. The caller was insistent that they meet that night, but Merlino was equally insistent, repeated that he would be in touch the moment he returned, and hung up. He took his client out to a very good dinner at a new French restaurant. As they come out of the restaurant, two men stepped out of the shadows to meet them. 'Mr Merlino, would you get into this car? Mr X of the Y insurance company wants to meet with you.' 'No, I'm terribly sorry, I can't do that.' 'Mr Merlino, I don't think you understand me,' came the reply. 'We insist.' The client said that he would take the licence plate of the car and report it to the hotel, so Merlino reluctantly got in with one man on either side of him. The car drove to a building near Red Square and he was ushered inside. There at the top of the steps was a middle-aged man who gave him two kisses on the cheek and the Russian bear hug.

'I'm sure you know why I asked you here tonight.'

'Asked?' said Merlino.

'We had to have this meeting.'

'Why?'

'Because of what you did today.'

'What did I do?'

'You met with the Deputy Prime Minister.'

'Yes.'

'You met with members of the City Council.'

'Yes.'

'You gave them a gift.'

'Yes.'

'What about a gift for me?'

Merlino took out a J&H pen from his jacket and handed it over. It was thrown on the floor. 'You know what I'm talking about.'

'No.'

'The gift.'

'What gift?'

'The personal commission – the money.'

'I didn't give them any money.'

'No one sees these people without bringing them a gift. I want one too. As soon as you agree to give me a gift, the meeting's over.'

Merlino thought very quickly. 'We are a very structured company, like yours, and I personally want to see that you get a gift, but I don't have the money. I'll talk to my board and ask them to send you a gift.'

The Russian thought about it, there was a lot of whispering, and then he said, 'That's acceptable – we'll take you home to the hotel.'

'No thank you,' said Merlino. 'I'll take a taxi.'

John Gussenhoven was not comfortable travelling to Russia, but the Russian team did manage to get him to go to Moscow once. He was very concerned about hygiene. Having a drink before dinner at the Kempinsky Hotel, Merlino ordered a Coca-Cola, so Gussenhoven ordered one too. 'John, you just made a serious mistake.' 'What did I do?' 'You forgot to say "No ice." '

'Waiter, waiter ...' cried Gussenhoven in a panic. They then went to a Georgian restaurant. Volker Preuss and Bruce Trigg were keen to try out all the new dishes, but Gussenhoven was reluctant. 'What's this, Paul?' 'How do we know this doesn't come from the Ukraine where there is all the radioactivity?' 'We don't, John, but I'm sure it's fine.' He didn't eat anything. When it came to say good-byes, a very senior man from one of the Russian insurance companies, who by this time was feeling no pain, came up to Gussenhoven. 'John, we always liked Dick Meyer. We respect you and consider you to be a colleague of ours.' With that he bent forward to give him a kiss, from which Gussenhoven recoiled in horror. Not to be outdone, and past caring about formalities, the Russian kept lunging at him, until he finally got his kiss.

Elsewhere in UNISON there were other changes afoot. When Mees & zoonen was brought by the ABN bank in 1962, it was clear that the bank was more interested in Mees's banking than its insurance broking interests. To ensure the future of Mees & zoonen as a leading Dutch global broker, Aad Strijbos persuaded ABN to sell to J&H. J&H acquired the entire company in 1990, apart from a small share held by the directors, but this was not announced till the following year.

One of the many complications arising from Willis's automatic expulsion from UNISON on the formation of Willis Corroon was the future of Boels & Bégault. Willis had acquired twenty per cent of the group in 1988, and UNISON was uncomfortable dealing with a partner who was partially owned by a competitor. In the event the board of Boels & Bégault entered into discussion with Bain Clarkson and Willis ended

John Gussenhoven

up selling their twenty per cent to the latter in 1992, who then acquired the entire group. At a later date, Bain Clarkson was in turn swallowed up by Aon. UNISON responded by setting up UNISON Belgium with a nucleus of ex Boels & Bégault people.

Elsewhere around the world, joint ventures in Canada and Australasia were unscrambled, and UNISON found new partners in Australia and New Zealand. Willis had also to be replaced in the United Arab Emirates, and the manager of J&H in Saudi recommended Gibbs Hartley Cooper in Dubai. After a three-day visit to Saudi, Ken Seward flew to Dubai to meet them. Being the keen golfer that he was, he had always been intrigued by the Emirates Golf Club – a green oasis built in a real desert irrigated by desalinated water at great expense to the Emir. As three of them went out to play, the 'pro' indicated that there was a woman who was looking for a game and asked if she could join them. They said sure, and her bag was put on Seward's cart. As there had been no time for lunch, he ordered a ham sandwich and a beer. The lady turned out to be a very attractive Eurasian in extremely short shorts. As he sat in his cart with pork, alcohol, and a scantily dressed woman who was not his wife, Seward marvelled at the thought of the reaction of the *Matawas* (the Saudi religious police) to finding so much evil in one small golf cart. How different are the countries of the Middle East.

To raise the profile of UNISON in Europe, Ken Seward, in his capacity as president of UNISON SA, relocated to Brussels and spent the next two years commuting between Belgium and New York. Luk van Berckelaer had been appointed to succeed Nick Davenport as manager. Luk being a very technically orientated and fastidious Belgian was one day reading through the UNISON charter that had been signed in Rome in 1987, only to discover that the term of office of the president was three years, with no second term. As Seward was still in office in 1992 and had every intention of remaining so till he retired at the end of 1993, the papers had to be changed and signed by all the partners. Asked why he had inserted that particular clause, the J&H lawyer who drew up the original document replied that it just seemed a good idea at the time.

After retiring from J&H at the end of 1995, Rudi Portaria was recalled as a consultant to assist with opening the new J&H office in Shanghai. This was a very special assignment for Rudi, because Shanghai was the city of his birth. He arrived in the spring of 1996 for a six-month stay. The office was a single room in a small seedy hotel adjacent to the Hilton. There was one other employee, Eva Guai, but within a week, two more arrived, seconded from the office in Hong Kong. They had to move. It didn't take him long to find wonderful premises away from the Shanghai Bund in a modern high-rise in what was once the French Concession in the colonial era – an area Rudi knew well, having lived and played there as a child.

The day of the move arrived, and looking out of the window, they saw the moving vehicle – a motor-cycle-driven flat-bed about fifteen foot long. 'Don't worry,' said Eva. 'That's how everyone moves in China.' The removers came in, and loaded everything on to the flat-bed. Desks, typewriters, books and papers, teapots and cups, J&H and UNISON plaques: everything was tied down and ready to go. 'Hold on, what about insurance?' said Rudi. No one had ever asked the movers about that before. They couldn't raise the J&H insurers so it was decided to self-insure, with the office staff escorting the flat-bed in two taxis for good measure.

As time went on Chip Bechtold took over the chairmanship of the PWG from Martin Rayner, who had in turn succeeded Bob Beane. Chip initiated the UNISON Round Tables. A small number of hand-picked prospective clients – one from each host country – were individually invited to attend a series of presentations, on topics that had been suggested beforehand by themselves, given by prominent UNISON experts at some interesting European location. The first Round Table was held in Venice in 1992. The opening event on Sunday evening was dinner in a beautiful room in the Danieli Hotel. On coming down to breakfast on Monday morning, it was discovered that the hotel reception and the whole of San Marco was flooded. The table and chairs in the meeting room had to be placed on duckboards, but the entire event was a great success, and served as a template for a regular succession of Round Tables.

FRATINI EN ACCION!
(WALDORF ASTORIA , N.Y.)

ER BARCAIZTEGUI
SPAIN

TO FRANCO
FROM
BARCA.
N.Y. April 81

Franco Fratini was due to give a presentation at one of these Round Tables at the Waldorf Astoria Hotel in New York, and was rehearsing his lines with Jim Hutchin the evening before. Through the lobby came an endless procession of simply stunning young ladies, absolutely dressed to the nines. Eventually, curiosity got the better of them, and Franco and Jim joined the next elevator complete with its animated cargo to see what was happening. The doors opened to find them back-stage at the New York pageant for the Miss America competition. In a flash they were surrounded by contestants, eager to know who they were. 'Ladies,' said Jim, 'this is Mr Fratini, the owner of the largest modelling agency in Milan.' It was the only time Jim Hutchin had ever known Franco Fratini to be left speechless.

Gussenhoven returned to New York in 1995 and was replaced as Chairman and CEO of J&H in Europe by Dan Jones. Unfortunately, David Olsen forgot to clear this with the UNISON partners beforehand, so he had rather a rough start. But he was immensely able, and went on to become vice-chairman of Marsh Inc., responsible for all non-North American operations. He also boasted ten children, which even took a leaf out of Bob Roberts's book.

Ever since the beginning of the 80s, the unsung heroes of J&H international had been the three team leaders who formed the backbone of the New York international department: Mike Heim, Joe Dell and Larry Templeman. Not only did they personally look after some of the largest international accounts, but they trained scores of future international people, many of whom were to become extremely successful. Heim and Dell had both come up the classic route of an overseas assignment and then returning to New York; Templeman had somehow always managed to avoid an overseas assignment and never left New York.

Outwardly, progress was still being made. J&H Ltd in London had got off to a very good start, and to give it even further international visibility, the 1994 UNISON conference was held at Gleneagles in Scotland. An agreement was signed committing all the UNISON partners to act together as a virtual company on international business, whilst maintaining their individual identities on domestic business. Ian Macalpine-Leny suggested renting a light aircraft towing a streamer announcing 'Willis Corroon welcomes you to Scotland' above the golf course during the regulation golf afternoon, but like many of the best ideas in life, the aircraft never got off the ground. 1995 was the hundred-and-fiftieth anniversary of the founding of Johnson & Higgins, and as part of the celebrations, the UNISON conference was held in Washington, DC. The very impressive book documenting the story of J&H to mark the event gave no inkling of what was to come.

By 1995, the PWG had evolved into the 'UNISON Change Team' under the leadership of Norman Barham, executive Vice-President of J&H. By then, Javier Barcaiztegui and Luc Malâtre had been joined by Martin Kessler, David Frediani (by then in J&H Italy), Ron Whyte (J&H Ltd in London), John Bonnor, Bruce Trigg from Jauch & Hübener, Peter Jägers from Mees & zoonen, and Rob Meyers and Bob Schram from J&H New York. This group focused on three pillars: a sales pillar lead by David Frediani, a global markets pillar led by Bruce Trigg, and a technical pillar led by Luc Malâtre.

But there was continuing frustration. Despite being now reduced to number three in terms of size after Marsh & McLennan and Aon, UNISON was still number one for client service. Everything at the operational level was fine, but there was a growing sense of paralysis. It was clear that the partners couldn't make a decision and then execute it. It was soon to become apparent why.

David Olsen

19 ... and Fall

The J&H directors had been very careful to monitor the progress of their competitors, and had always been concerned that J&H, because of its private status, would ultimately prove to be at a disadvantage. Even at the time that Marsh & McLennan went public, the board had a fierce debate as to whether or not J&H should follow suit. By the beginning of the 1990s, it was all too apparent that J&H was continuing to lose ground to Marsh. This was the time of the incredible expansion of Aon who, driven by the dynamic Pat Ryan, went from being an obscure US broker to the world's largest global broker after Marsh & McLennan in the space of ten years.

As so often when a major organisation is faced with indecision, J&H called in McKinsey. Bob Hatcher had been succeeded in 1991 by David Olsen, whose father Al Olsen had been a J&H director. Olsen was a very different man from Hatcher. He had joined J&H's marine department in San Francisco in 1966 from the Great American Insurance Company. He had never been in favour of a merger with Willis, and enthusiastically supported the initiative to convert J&H Ltd into a viable London retail broker. McKinsey recommended among other things that the US international departments should be absorbed into the property department. Ken Seward had retired at the end of 1993, and Martin Rayner moved from the international department in New York to head up the Salt Lake City office, leaving Bob Beane as the only international director in New York. John Gussenhoven, originally a property director, had succeeded Seward as president of UNISON SA and so head of global international.

By 1996, the J&H directors had lost faith in the future. Marsh and Aon continued to consolidate with Aon announcing the acquisition of Alexander & Alexander, while in UNISON there wasn't enough pressure for change. UNISON couldn't evolve, because there was resistance to change in Europe, and lack of leadership from J&H. With the benefit of hindsight, it was clear that J&H had made strategic mistakes in the past, not going into reinsurance despite the entreaties of Willis Faber in the 1930s being the most serious. Not taking a more professional approach to employee benefits much sooner was another. But what ultimately weighed most heavily on the performance of J&H was, with one or two notable exceptions, the declining quality of the directors. The policy of always recruiting from within, a noble but risky intention at the best of times, had finally taken its toll. The only director recruited from outside was Joe Roxe, who came in from Mobil Oil in 1988 as chief financial officer.

During 1996, the directors brought in Morgan Stanley in addition to McKinsey to study the competitive environment. The global brokerage business was healthy and J&H's short-term future was strong. But faced with industry consolidation and enormous requirements for capital to fund both technology and expansion, J&H's private ownership presented constraints that threatened its long-term future.

In addition, J&H had been having their own leadership problems, not helped by the fact that David Olsen and Dick Nielsen were both due to retire in the same year. Of the four executive vice-presidents from whom would normally come the next chairman and president, Bob Powell had died and John Gussenhoven and Joe Platt had lost the confidence of their fellow directors. After a full meeting of the board, Norman Barham was elected president and held that position for the year prior to the sale of the company.

The directors considered the options available. Obviously the first was to go public, but that would leave J&H vulnerable to any passing predator. The next was to sell to another broker, and a number, but not Willis Corroon, were approached. The third was to buy another broker. The last was to do a deal with a bank. Marsh & McLennan was never even considered. Then in October 1996, a team came back and reported to the board that they had had a very good meeting with Marsh. You could hear a pin drop. 'Holy shit, what does that mean?' Everyone had always thought that Marsh would never be interested. But Marsh thought it would be a great combination. There was no talk of acquisition, rather of a merger, and Marsh were open to whatever J&H wanted to do.

184

It had always been assumed by previous boards of J&H that the company wasn't theirs to sell, and they had a duty to pass it on to the next generation in better shape than they had found it. The by-laws clearly stated that the shares could only go to existing employees, every retiring director receiving in return for transferring his shares to his successor on the board a certificate entitling him to receive income from the firm for a period of ten years after retirement. But legally the directors could sell the company, although they had to change the by-laws to allow for the shares to pass outside the firm. The news broke on Wednesday 12 March 1997. The employees of J&H worldwide were absolutely shattered, and felt they had been sold down the river.*

The UNISON Steering Committee, as the PWG was by then called, were preparing for a Round Table in the Hotel Albatroz in Lisbon when the news came through from New York. There was nothing to do but cancel all the guests, pack up the handouts, and try and have a good dinner. Javier Barcaiztegui couldn't sleep that night. There were albatrosses pecking at his window like something out of Hitchcock's *The Birds*.

Sitting in London, Macalpine-Leny was immensely puzzled that the J&H board was reported as being unanimous in accepting this deal, knowing as he did that Christian Dahms, Patrick Lucas and Santi Gil de Biedma had all been elected to the board in 1995. Surely they wouldn't have voted for this? A phone call to Luc Malâtre in Paris the next day revealed the surprising truth that the three UNISON directors had not even been at the board meeting. They had been told that it was only routine and they didn't need to attend, so had never been consulted.† They were incandescent, especially Santi Gil, who had sold fifty per cent of Gil y Carvajal's shares to J&H in what he understood

* Twenty-five per cent of the proceeds of the sale was distributed among the top ten per cent of the staff, who were thought to have a good future with the new company. It was thought that the cultures of the two companies would be similar, but because of one being a private and the other a public company, they were very different. This proved harder on the J&H-ers than expected.
† The real reasons were that they didn't have stock ownership in J&H, and as Marsh was a public company, it would have been against Stock Exchange regulations.

was a deal for life. After discussion, they reluctantly agreed to fly to New York, but it was a wasted trip – it was too late.

Patrick Lucas called the European UNISON partners to Paris to discuss what they should do next. Patrick wanted to reconstitute UNISON. It was agreed that they should approach the key players likely to be interested in a deal: Marsh, Willis, Sedgwick and Aon. On learning the news of the fallout in Europe from J&H's sale to Marsh, Macalpine-Leny immediately notified his chairman that this presented a huge opportunity, and recommended that Willis should make a play for first Jauch & Hübener, then Gras Savoye, and then Gil y Carvajal. Approaches were immediately made to both Jauch & Hübener and Gras Savoye. Gil y Carvajal were in the difficult position that fifty per cent of their shares were now owned by Marsh.

Bob Beane had been in an unusual position because he had agreed in the spring of 1995 to take early retirement from the board of J&H in early 1997. However, it soon became clear that John Gussenhoven, although the director of international, had no detailed knowledge of the UNISON network, so Beane was asked to stay on. One minute he was clearing his desk, the next he was right in the thick of the negotiations. After the deed was done, Gil y Carvajal reminded J&H that they had an agreement to buy back their shares if circumstances changed, but Marsh would have none of it. It was only when it became clear that in no way would Gil y Carvajal report to Marsh's much smaller Spanish operation, run by a Chilean, that they agreed to reconsider. Beane and Roxe went over to strike a deal with Santi, which they did, but when they returned to New York, they were over-ruled by Marsh. Gil y Carvajal eventually bought back their shares for a higher price.

Meanwhile, the J&H directors had run into all sorts of trouble with the retired directors, and the whole sorry tale of the subsequent law suits was there for all to see in the pages of the *Wall Street Journal*. Basically, the directors had agreed to keep fifty per cent of the proceeds of the sale for themselves, give twenty-five per cent to the employees, and twenty-five per cent spread between the certificate holder directors, and those directors who had been retired for more than ten years.* With the benefit of hindsight, David Olsen knew that if he had consulted Dick Purnell and Bob Hatcher at the beginning, things might have gone much more smoothly and some of the more obvious pitfalls might have been avoided.

Back in Europe, Patrick Lucas kept his promise to the Gras Savoye employees that a decision on the future of Gras Savoye would be made by Bastille Day, 14 July, and announced that a minority stake would be sold to Willis with an option to increase to a majority at 30 December 2009. Always one jump ahead of the game, Patrick had long since got control of the company from the non-executive shareholders. When John Reeve, who had succeeded Roger Elliot as chairman of Willis in 1995, came over to have dinner with Patrick after the deal was announced, he explained that he hadn't been able to tell him before that Willis was in negotiations to sell to either Marsh or Sedgwick or Kohlberg, Kravis, Roberts (KKR), the leverage buy-out specialists. Patrick, yet again holding the trump card, reminded Reeve that the Willis deal with Gras Savoye would be null and void if Willis sold out to a competitor. Fortunately, that wasn't to happen.†

Meanwhile, Jauch & Hübener had been negotiating with Marsh & McLennan for three months. Marsh had a pre-emptive option to buy Jauch & Hübener, but as they insisted that their German company, which was at the time only two-thirds the size of Jauch & Hübener, should be in the driving seat, and therefore head up the merged German company, Jauch & Hübener broke off the negotiations and contacted Aon. Aon

* The basis of the law suit brought by the majority of the certificate holders was that (i) they believed that they should have been included in the decision-making, which would have been impossible given the confidentiality necessary due to Marsh being a public company; and (ii) they were entitled to a larger share of the proceeds.

† KKR, supported by five leading insurance companies, led a cash offer in 1998 recommended by the Willis Corroon board to acquire all the shares of Willis Corroon, thereby taking the company private again. When Willis was brought back to the stock market in 2001 by means of an Independent Public Offering, this proved to have been one of the best investments KKR had ever made.

was not well known to them, but Pat Ryan, being a great sales-man, convinced the partners that a deal would be the best course for the firm.

Christian Dahms then introduced Santi Gil de Biedma to Pat Ryan, and as a result, Gil y Carvajal also concluded a deal with Aon. John Bonnor had meanwhile sold out to Marsh, as had Max Matthiessen. The wily Swiss, on the other hand, bought Marsh's retail operation in Switzerland and sold them only twenty-five per cent of Kessler. Marsh presumably agreed to this when faced with losing yet another member of the UNISON network.

It was all over.

Peter Jägers

20 Epilogue

Today, UNISON is best known as the name of the largest trade union in the UK, and Johnson and Higgins, once the world's largest privately owned insurance broker and one of the oldest and proudest names in the insurance industry, has ceased to exist. Its people have been swallowed up by the survivors in the business, and its records, like its art collection, have disappeared without trace.

Mike Heim was strolling through the Upper East Side of New York one day when there, staring out at him from the windows of a thrift (charity) shop, were the portraits of Henry Ward Johnson and Andrew Foster Higgins that once proudly adorned the walls of the board room. In utter disbelief that such a thing could have happened, he hurriedly snapped them up, and they now have pride of place in his dining room.

But the spirit of UNISON lives on. The people described in these pages sustain that common bond of friendship, forged while working closely together for so many years, by getting together from time to time around the world to eat and drink and tell stories of the old days. This book, no doubt, will add to them.

Appendix I The Players

† Taped interview for this book
* Provided written or verbal material

THE FIRMS

Boels & Bégault – UNISON partner for Belgium. Sold to Bain Clarkson (and subsequently Aon), 1992.

Bonnor & Co – UNISON partner for Denmark. Sold to Marsh, 1997.

Brockman y Schuh – UNISON partner for Mexico. Sold 50 per cent to J&H. Subsequently sold to Marsh.

Costa Duarte & Lima – UNISON partner for Portugal until replaced by Boels & Bégault Portugal, 1984.

Gil y Carvajal – UNISON partner for Spain. J&H acquired 25 per cent 1989, increased to 50 per cent 1991. Sold to Aon, 1997.

Gras Savoye – UNISON partner for France from 1975. Minority interest sold to Willis 1997.

Jauch & Hübener – UNISON partner for Germany. Sold to Aon, 1997.

Johnson & Higgins – UNISON partner for USA and Italy. Sold to Marsh, 1997.

Kessler & Co – UNISON partner for Switzerland. Minority interest sold to Marsh, 1997.

Max Matthiessen – UNISON partner for Sweden from 1984. Sold to Marsh, 1997.

Mees & zoonen – UNISON partner for The Netherlands. Acquired by J&H, 1990.

Mercury Insurance Agencies – UNISON partner for Greece. Sold to Gras Savoye, 1994.

SGCA – UNISON partner for France until sold controlling stake to Reed Stenhouse and replaced by Gras Savoye, 1975.

Willis Faber – UNISON partner for the UK until the formation of Willis Corroon in 1990.

THE PEOPLE

Anthony, Charles (Charlie) – Joined J&H New York property department, 1964. Transferred to J&H Italy in Milan as manager 1968, returning to J&H in Hartford 1973. Resigned *circa* 1975. p. 83, 84, 136

Barcaiztegui, Javier† – Joined Gil y Carvajal Madrid international department 1972. International manager and member of PWG 1979. Elected to the board 1985. p. 73, 75, 102, 108, 110, 112, 185

Barham, Norman – Joined J&H New York 1975. Director, 1987. Executive vice-president 1992. Chairman UNISON operations committee, 1995. President, 1996; vice-chairman, Marsh & McLennan, 1997. Retired 2000. p. 182, 184

Barrett, Michael (Mike)† – Joined Gras Savoye international department 1978. Country manager, Cameroons, 1988; manager, new business unit, Paris, 1992; opened Vietnam office, 1994; returned to Paris, 1998. p. 66, 67, 102

Beane, S. Robert (Bob)† – Joined J&H Philadelphia employee benefits department 1967. Resigned 1969. Joined Gil y Carvajal 1969 Madrid, setting up employee benefits and then international department. Founder member PWG. Rejoined J&H 1979 as manager of J&H Italy; manager New York international department 1984 and chairman PWG. Director 1987. Retired 1997. p. 73, 87, 106, 179, 183, 186

Bechtold, Charles H. Jnr (Chip)† – Joined J&H New York 1976; international manager 1980. Transferred to Milan 1984 as country manager Italy; New York 1990; J&H UK Ltd. London, 1991. New York 1994, regional manager, Latin America. Member of PWG 1982–1990 and 1992–1994. Retired 1997. p. 64, 87, 170, 179

Bégault, Emile – Founded Boels & Bégault 1920, with brother-in-law Fritz Boels, then an insurance agent for Assurances Générale. President 1958. President of the professional association of Belgian insurance brokers for many years. Died 1970. p. 23, 77, 88, 97

Bégault, Lucien Emile Madeleine Louise (Lucien) – Joined Boels & Bégault from industry 1957 as partner in charge of finance and administration. Elected president 1976. Died 1986. p. 89, 90

Benedict, Lloyd† – Joined J&H New York property department from AFIA 1959. Opened J&H Italy 1964. Returned New York to head the international department 1966. Director 1972. Retired 1984. p. 19, 33, 56, 63, 72, 77, 79, 80, 97

Bickett, Peter B. (Pete)* – Joined J&H New York property department 1954. Responsibility for 'foreign section' (forerunner of international department) 1956. Milan (1966) and Brussels (1967) to co-ordinate J&H European business, returning to New York in

1968. Manager of international department 1970. Founding member and first chairman of PWG. Director 1979. Retired 1985. p. 20, 31, 33, 99, 105, 107, 112

Binford, Charles (Charlie)* – Joined J&H in 1973 as manager, Phoenix, Arizona. Manager Willis Faber J&H, Sydney, Australia, 1982. President J&H Japan 1985. New York 1993. Retired in 1994. p. 137, 138, 145, 156

Bonnor, John† – Joined Baltica in 1960, training in UK and New Zealand. Set up Bonnor & Co. 1979; founder member of Danish brokers association, 1980; UNISON partner for Denmark 1982. p. 93, 94, 182, 188

Bumsted, William J. (Bill)* – Joined J&H after graduation from Dartmouth. Manager, J&H Venezuela, 1956. Returned to New York 1961 as manager of the marine cargo department and overseas offices. Director 1962. Retired 1979. p. 16, 21, 89

Cameron, Robert A. (Bob)* – Joined J&H to open the Boston office with George Shattuck in 1963. Director 1977. Retired 1990. p. 35, 36, 153

Camp, Glenn T.* – Joined J&H in New York 1978. Country manager Saudi Arabia 1981 to 1984. International practice leader for Marsh in Philadelphia. p. 142–144

Carega, Paolo* – Joined J&H Boston as trainee 1969; transferred to New York. Opened Rome office jointly with Italo Maffei 1972; transferred to Gras Savoye, Paris, 1975; international manager, J&H Washington, DC, 1982. Resigned and joined Marsh & McLennan, 1988. p. 64, 84

Cartmell, Jennifer* – Assistant treasurer, Marsh & McLennan Inc., 1984; Corroon & Black Corp., 1985; first vice-president, treasurer and development officer, 1988 and for Willis Corroon, 1990. Chief operating officer, Willis Corroon, New York, 1992. Resigned, 1993 to move to Heddington Insurance Ltd (Texaco), Bermuda. p. 165, 167

Claydon, Michael† – Joined Willis 1962. Progressed through fire survey department to administration director then managing director of London retail company. Represented Willis Corroon in New York 1993 to 1995. p. 49

Cohen, Jeremy S.* – Joined Willis Faber in London 1961. Managing director Willis Faber Advisory Services 1970; life director 1972; main board director 1984; retired 1988. p. 103

Crawford, Peter H.† – Joined Willis Sheffield 1972; managing director of Willis Sheffield, 1987; retired 1999. p. 134

Crook, Humphrey L.* – Joined J&H Cleveland 1973, transferring to

J&H St Louis 1978 to start the property department. Retired 2000 and now doing consultancy work for Marsh. p. 153

Dahms, Christian† – Joined Jauch & Hübener 1965. 12 months training with J&H New York in 1968, returning to Germany 1969 as manager of international department. Founding member of the PWG. Partner Jauch & Hübener, 1984; spokesman of the board, 1989. Director J&H 1995. Retired, 2001. p. 55, 59, 96, 106, 110, 149, 159, 167, 185, 188

Dalzell, Richard† – Joined Willis Faber from Trafalgar House as finance director-elect in 1988. Main board director 1989; finance director Willis Corroon 1994; resigned 1997. p. 164, 166

Davenport, Nicholas P. (Nick)† – Joined Willis Faber in London 1971. First manager Willis Faber Boels & Bégault, Brussels 1973. Paris 1976 to open Gras Savoye Willis Faber. Willis London 1980, responsible for reinsurance in French-speaking Africa and Greece. Manager, UNISON SA, 1989 (resigned 1990); managing director Willis Corroon Europe, 1990; chairman Willis Corroon France, 1995. Resigned 1998. p. 161, 162, 166, 168

Day, Michael G.† – Joined Willis Faber in London 1955 and serviced J&H multinational clients in UK and Europe from 1959. Attended first UNISON conference in 1965; life director Willis Faber 1971 and managing director, overseas department, 1980. Retired 1985. p. 20, 47, 61, 71, 77, 90, 98, 102, 103, 121

DeFoe, Karl – Joined J&H Detroit international department 1969. Transferred to Cleveland as international manager 1973. J&H Singapore 1982. International manager, J&H Philadelphia, 1984. New York international department 1985. Retired 1998. p. 101

Dell, Joseph T (Joe)* – Joined J&H New York 1966 and transferred to international 1968. J&H Singapore 1974. New York international department 1976. Retired 1994. p. 99, 139, 173, 181

Dowd, Edmund J. (Ed)* – Joined J&H Los Angles from AIG in 1966; started international department. Transferred to Singapore and became manager 1974. Retired 1986; rehired to perform legal audits of 29 J&H offices in 17 countries. p. 139

Elliott, Roger J.† – Joined Willis Faber marine department in 1950. Life director, 1971. Chairman, marine division then aviation division. Chairman, 1988; retired 1995. p. 164, 166, 167, 168

Faber, Julian T. – Son of Alfred Faber, one of eight original partners of Willis, Faber & Co. Joined 1939; served in World War II; life director, 1954; joint deputy-chairman, 1969; chairman, 1972; retired 1977; died 2002. p. 44, 46, 50

Faiers, Michael C. (Mike)† – Served in World War II. Rejoined small Lloyd's broker, rising to managing director. Insurance manager, GKN, 1970, becoming corporate staff director – risk management. Retired 1984; consultant to Willis Faber for 5 years. p. 57, 58, 121

Faison, Seth* – Joined J&H New York in 1958 as vice-president and secretary of the new business committee with responsibility for sales training and advertising. Retired 1989. p. 111, 130

Franklin-Adams, Patrick† – Head-hunted to be chairman and first employee of J&H (UK) Ltd, London, 1991. Resigned 1997. p. 170

Frediani, David† – Joined J&H San Francisco 1981; New York 1982. Resident vice-president, Brockman y Schuh, Mexico, 1984; country manager Malaysia 1988; Milan branch manager and UOC member for Italy 1993; J&H (UK) Ltd, London, 1995; head of geographical development, Marsh & McLennan Comps. Inc., 2003. p. 156, 182

Fratini, Franco* – Joined J&H Italy (Milan) in 1972 as account manager. Appointed branch manager (Rome) in 1980; country manager in 1988; chairman and chief executive officer of J&H Italy, 1990. Retired 2001. p. 87, 180

Gil de Biedma, Santiago (Santi)† – Joined Gil y Carvajal in 1958. Managing director 1963. Attended every UNISON conference from the first in Brussels in 1965. Chairman 1973. Director, J&H, 1995. p. 47, 71, 75, 150, 159, 185, 186, 188

Gortazar, Fernando – Joined Gil y Carvajal, Madrid commercial department in 1978, rising to deputy manager of the department in 1987. International manager 1992, retaining this position through G y C's merger with Aon. p. 150

Gregory, Adrian A.* – Joined Willis Faber in London 1968. Chairman UK retail company 1979; main board director 1980; deputy-chairman 1988. Retired 1993. p. 32, 48, 58, 161, 165, 166, 167, 170

Groene, Jack – Joined J&H Venezuela in 1958 following J&H acquisition of his family-owned brokerage business in Puerto la Cruz. Caracas, 1961; president, 1964 until retirement in 1989. p. 16

Groth, Göran – Joined Max Matthiessen in Stockholm 1965. Became sole owner, managing director and president in 1975 and moved the firm from being correspondent of Marsh & McLennan to member of UNISON in 1984. Sold Max Matthiessen to Marsh, 1997. p. 104

Gussenhoven, John – Joined J&H New York property department 1977. Director 1989; chairman & CEO, J&H Europe, 1992; president of UNISON 1994; returned to New York, 1995; resigned following sale to Marsh, 1997. p. 172, 175, 181, 183, 186

Guthrie, Robert B. (Bob)* – Joined Willis Faber in 1958. Fire manager,

Bristol, 1965. J&H team with Ken Withers in London, 1968. Managing director, UK retail company, 1988; retired 2002. p. 153, 154

Harlow, James G. – Joined J&H employee benefits department 1960. Director 1975; first managing director New York branch 1982; retired 1988. p. 123, 129

Hatcher, Robert V. Jnr (Bob)† – Partner in a Richmond, Virginia, insurance agency, Baker-Cotterell. Opened J&H office in Richmond when J&H acquired Baker-Cotterell. Director 1975; moved to New York as president, 1977; chairman & CEO 1982. Retired 1990. p. 102, 129, 145, 148, 149, 163, 165, 167, 187

Hausman, Hugh – Joined J&H Venezuela (Caracas) from AFIA in 1966. Resident vice-president at SGCA Paris, 1968. Oversaw transfer of entire J&H account to new UNISON partner Gras Savoye in 1975. Seconded to United Iranian Insurance Services, Tehran, in 1978; returned to New York, 1979. Retired, 1991. Died 2001. p. 63, 65, 67, 106, 133, 134, 141, 150, 151, 156, 158, 173

van der Have, Wim – Joined Mees & zoonen in 1950. Founder-member of PWG. Opened Mees office in Djakarta, Indonesia, 1977. Retired 1985. Died 1989. p. 106

Heim, Michael (Mike)* – Joined J&H Chicago international department 1969. Assistant manager J&H Tokyo 1971; returned to New York 1974. Retired 1997 following J&H merger with Marsh & McLennan. p. 137, 181, 189

Henshaw, Richard T. Jnr (The General) – Started with J&H New York in 1954. In 1960 sent to J&H Detroit as branch manager, returning to New York 1962 as assistant to CEO Dorrance Sexton. Director 1963; executive vice-president 1966. Retired 1977. Died 1979. p. 44, 97

Hollmeyer, Harry W. – Opened J&H Brazil in 1954 and managed company until retired 1983. Died 1997. p. 16

Holloway, George R.* – Joined J&H New York marine cargo department, 1949, later moving to foreign credit. Resigned 1982. p.36

Hoshine, Takeo – Joined J&H in Tokyo, 1974; transferred to New York 1980. Retired 2003. p. 123

Hübener, Harald – Son of Jauch & Hübener founder, Otto Hübener, joined the firm in 1953. First trainee with J&H, New York, 1956. Manager Frankfurt office, 1964; transferred to Hamburg; partner 1971; spokesman of board, 1988. Died 1989. p. 55, 100, 103, 107, 149

Hübener, Oswald (Oschi) – Nephew of Otto Hübener, joined Jauch & Hübener in 1930s. Trained in Brazil and USA where interned on Ellis Island during Second World War. Partner 1951; retired 1981. Died 1994. p. 22, 55, 57, 58, 93, 100

Hutchin, James W. (Jim)* – Joined J&H San Francisco, 1979; New York, 1980. J&H representative Brockman y Schuh, Mexico, 1981. Sales manager, J&H Singapore, 1984; international manager, J&H Philadelphia, 1985; Milan branch manager, J&H Italy, 1990; New York corporate international, 1993; resigned 1994 to join Willis Corroon. p. 73, 87, 180

Jones, Brian W.† – Joined J&H Willis Faber, Toronto, 1975. Vice-president international and risk management, 1982; Toronto branch manager, 1989; director, 1995. Resigned following sale to Marsh to set up Jones Brown Inc. 1997. p. 124, 125

Jones, Daniel L. (Dan)* – Joined J&H in 1986 as branch manager in Salt Lake City, Utah. Co-manager New York branch, 1993; chairman & CEO, J&H Europe, 1995; vice-chairman Marsh Inc., 2002; resigned, 2003. p. 181

Kadri, George J. – J&H Detroit. Transferred to New York as international manager, 1977. New York corporate staff, 1980; managing principal, 1994; retired, 1997. p. 100

Karter, Jerome (Jerry)† – Joined J&H New York in 1984 from INA. International manager 1985. Resigned 1989 to become president of SCOR USA. p. 160

Kervyn de Meerendré, Daniel (Dany)† – Joined Boels & Bégault in 1955. Elected to the board 1970 as partner responsible for international. Founding member of PWG. 'Administrateur Délégué' of UNISON SA. Retired December 1990. p. 47, 89, 101, 106, 159

Kessler, Hans – Headed Kessler & Co., Switzerland from 1956 through 1986. Negotiated the co-operation of Kessler with Johnson & Higgins in 1965. Retired 1986. p. 94

Kessler, Martin* – Elder son of Hans Kessler; joined Kessler & Co., Zurich in 1978. Sent to J&H New York 1980, returning to Kessler, 1982. Managing partner, 1986. p. 94, 126, 182

Kessler, Robert – Younger son of Hans Kessler; joined Kessler 1979. 12 months training with Hartford Steam Boiler, 1982; returned to Kessler, Zurich, 1983. p. 94

Klapwijk, Arnold A. – Joined Mees & zoonen in Rotterdam, 1969. First Mees resident representative with J&H New York, 1983. Resigned, 1986. p. 127

Kratovil, Emil A. – Joined J&H 1966. Retired 1979. Rejoined Wilcox and finally retired, 1983. Died 2004. p. 130–132

Kratz, Corinna† – Joined Jauch & Hübener 1978. 12 months training, J&H Chicago; returned Jauch & Hübener, Mülheim. Resigned 1987; rejoined 1990. Resident representative J&H New York 1990. International department manager, Mülheim, 1993; resigned 1997. p. 127

Kronberger, Eugen F.* – Joined Jauch & Hübener Austria, 1972. United Iranian Insurance Services, Tehran, 1978. Escaped back to Germany via Turkey, 1979. South East Asian regional representative for Jauch & Hübener in Singapore, 1981. Corporate international department Mülheim, 1990. Retired 2004. p. 133, 134

Lahno, Ewald – Joined Jauch & Hübener in 1940s; served in World War II; partner 1963; spokesman of the board, 1974; retired 1986. p. 55, 58, 118

Ledger, Peter C. W.* – Joined Willis Faber's Sheffield office 1971. Responsible for UNISON business, both outgoing and incoming. Transferred to London 1987; responsible for large corporate accounts, and the substantial Willis Japanese retail account. Retired 2003. p. 152, 154

Lucas, Patrick† – Joined Gras Savoye in Paris in 1965 with responsibility for international insurance after 12 months training with UK brokers. Took part with his father, Max Lucas, in initial discussions with J&H in 1975; started Gras Savoye's international network. CEO, 1973; chairman and CEO, 1979. Director J&H, 1995. p. 62, 63, 185, 186, 187

Macalpine-Leny, Ian H. – Joined Willis in 1972. First Willis resident representative with J&H New York 1980 to 1983. Succeeded Ronnie Westhorp on PWG 1984. Retired 1999. p. 45, 108, 121, 125, 126, 127, 161, 167, 181, 185

Maffei, Italo – Joined J&H Italy in Milan, 1965. Co-manager with Paolo Carega of newly opened Rome office, 1972. J&H Detroit, 1978 as manager international department, returning to Milan in 1983. Resigned in 1989. p. 80, 84, 87

Malâtre, Luc† – Joined Gras Savoye Paris 1974. Manager, Tehran office, 1978; resident representative at J&H in New York, 1979. Returned Paris, 1983 responsible for marine aviation & credit, international 1990, reinsurance 2000. Joined PWG 1990; group executive committee 2001. p. 119, 121, 134, 182, 185

Merlino, Paul† – Joined J&H Atlanta 1986; transferred to Philadelphia, 1987; J&H UK Ltd in London, 1991; Joined team responsible for joint J&H/Jauch Hübener company in Moscow, 1994. Transferred to Marsh, Dallas, 2000. Resigned 2002. p. 170–176

Monahan, Catherine (Cathy)* – Joined J&H New York international reverse-flow unit, 1980, transferring in 1981 to the branch international department. Resigned 1990 to join SCOR. p. 150, 151

Olsen, David – Son of a retired J&H director, joined J&H San

Francisco marine department in 1966, transferring to Chicago as marine manager 1971. Branch manager Houston 1979; director 1986. New York 1985 as executive vice-president; chairman and CEO, 1991. p. 183, 187

Palmer, David V.† – Joined Willis Faber from Edward Lumley in New York in 1959. Life director 1969; deputy-chairman 1972; chairman, 1982; retired 1988. p. 48, 62, 90, 98, 102, 146, 147, 163, 165, 170

Pinkham, Paul – Joined J&H in New York about 1952. J&H Cuba until office closed 1960. Area specialist for Latin America, New York international department; country manager, Peru, 1985; retired 1990. p. 15, 34, 35

Portaria, Rudi† – Joined J&H Montreal, 1961. Assistant manager J&H Milan, 1964. New York, 1972; J&H European co-ordinator in Brussels, 1973. Founding member of PWG. Returned to New York 1978 as European area specialist. Retired 1994. Re-engaged by J&H to help develop the Shanghai office, 1996. p. 77, 82, 83, 95, 99, 101, 102, 106, 137, 152, 179

Purnell, Richard I (Dick) – Joined J&H Philadelphia in 1946 as trainee in marine department. Manager Pittsburgh office 1954 through 1961. Returned to J&H Philadelphia as manager in 1962 and was appointed to the board the same year. President, 1970; chairman and CEO, 1972; retired 1981. Died 2003. p. 30, 62, 82, 99, 105, 128, 139, 149, 163

Rainoff, George† – Joined J&H New York 1965. Opened J&H Tokyo, 1968; opened J&H Singapore 1972; New York, 1974; Beirut, 1975; Rome, 1975; Athens, 1976; Gras Savoye, Paris, 1978. Returned to New York 1981 with responsibility for business development Asia and Middle East. Retired 1991. p. 68, 106, 136, 138, 140–143, 145

Rayner, Martin L. – Joined J&H in Los Angeles, 1972. International department manager 1974; country manager Japan, 1983; returned to New York 1985 to become international practice leader and subsequently chairman of PWG. Director, 1987; branch manager, Salt Lake City, 1994; died 1994. p. 137, 179, 183

Regamey, Jean Claude – Chairman of SGCA, the original J&H correspondent in France. Died about 1988. p. 61

Riestra, Raymundo – Joined Gil y Carvajal Madrid 1978. Manager financial division, 1986. North-west regional manger, 1993. Resigned, 1999. p. 151

Roberts, Robert S. (Bob)* – Joined J&H New York casualty department, 1956. Retired as deputy casualty manager, 1986. p. 56, 181

Robins, John† – Joined main board of Willis Faber as finance director,

1984. Finance director, Willis Corroon, 1991. Resigned to become CEO of Guardian Royal Exchange Insurance Company, 1994. p. 164, 166

Roscoe, E. John T. – Joined Willis Faber, 1949 and was responsible for building the aviation division. Life director, 1959; chairman 1967. Retired 1972; died 1984. p. 41, 44, 146, 163

van de Sande, Gert† – Joined Mees & zoonen 1975. Succeeded Wim Nagelmakers on PWG 1982. Left UOC 1995. Retired 2001. p. 92

Satrústegui, Patricio (Paddy) – Joined Gil y Carvajal 1967. Regional manager 1970; director, 1976; deputy chairman, 1978; non-executive director, 2001. p. 72

Sautière, Claude† – Joined Gras Savoye in Paris, 1968. Opened Tehran office, 1975; transferred to J&H New York 1978, returning to Paris 1979 to become international manager. Deputy managing director 1986. Succeeded Henri Sommer on PWG. Resigned 1996. p. 68, 108, 109, 119, 127

Schauff, Dietrich† – Joined Jauch & Hübener, Hamburg, 1960, transferring to Mülheim in 1963. After 12 months training in UK, returned to Germany 1967, becoming property manager. International department manager, Frankfurt, 1978; first resident representative with J&H New York, 1979; resident vice-president, Willis Faber Enthoven, Johannesburg, South Africa, 1984. International manager, Mülheim, 1987. Co-manager of Frankfurt branch, 1988, when joined PWG. Retired 2000. p. 108, 118, 119, 123, 124

Scheller, Heidi* – Joined J&H in Boston, 1978. Resigned 1993 to join Willis Corroon; resigned, 1998. p. 153

Schram, Robert L. (Bob)* – Joined J&H New York international department 1976; J&H Brazil, 1980; deputy international manager, New York, 1986. Manager, São Paulo, Brazil, 1990; New York, 1994 as manager international practice office and member of UNISON Change Team/UNISON Operating Committee; resigned from Marsh 2000. p. 173, 182

Seward, J. Kenneth (Ken)† – Joined J&H New York in 1959. Maracaibo, 1960; Caracas, 1965; general manager J&H Colombia, 1966. Managing director J&H Italy, 1973. Founding member of PWG. Returned to New York 1979 as manager overseas subsidiaries. Director 1982. First president of UNISON SA, 1987; resident Brussels 1990 to 1993. Retired December 1993. p. 17, 35, 85, 96, 106, 128, 144, 159, 177, 183

Sexton, Dorrance – Son of a serving J&H director, joined J&H New York in 1933. Served in World War II. Director 1949. Succeeded

Elmer Jefferson as president in 1960; chairman and CEO 1962. Retired 1972. Died 1987. p. 15, 18, 35, 44, 77, 99, 100, 135, 136, 146, 163

Slade, David N. – Joined Willis Faber in London, 1965. Resident wholesaling representative with J&H New York, 1987 to 1990. Retired 1991; died 1993. p. 92, 122

Sommer, Henri* – Joined Gras Savoye in Paris as manager of international department, 1973. Founding member of PWG. New business manager, 1980; resigned 1984. p. 66, 67, 106

South, Anthony J. (Tony) – Joined Willis Faber in London, 1970. Manager, United Iranian Insurance Services, Tehran, 1977. Returned to London, 1979. Resigned 1987. p. 134

Steele, Michael (Ms)* – Joined J&H New York 1978 as secretary to foreign representatives. Personal assistant to Jim Harlow 1982. Resigned 1988. p. 123

Stephenson, Patrick J. T. (Paddy) – Joined Dupuis, Parizeau, Tremblay in Montreal, Canada (acquired by J&H, 1958). President, J&H Canada, 1963; chairman, J&H Willis Faber, 1973; chairman, J&H Ltd, Bermuda, 1977; retired 1984; died 2003. p. 21, 22, 78, 79

Strijbos, Aad S.* – Joined Mees & zoonen in 1962 as trainee; property department director after six months. 1968, manager property and liability departments and Amsterdam office. Executive board 1988 and chairman 1989. Managing principal, J&H, 1994; retired 2002. p. 91, 92, 176

Tarpohzy, Demitri (Taky) – Founded Tarpohzy & Co. (general agents for AFIA) in Athens in early 1960s, and Mercury Insurance Agencies in 1965. Finally retired in 2003. p. 95

Taylor, A. R. (Ronnie)* – Joined Willis Faber in 1959 to run employee benefits. Took over UK retail company, 1965; life director and main board director, 1965; chairman 1978; retired 1981. p. 46, 48, 84, 99, 163

Templeman, Lawrence I., II (Larry)* – Joined J&H in 1964 in domestic property department. Joined J&H international department in 1970. Client manager for many large global accounts. Retired in 1997. p. 181

Thomson, F. K. (Tommy)* – Joined Willis Faber's fire department in London 1938. Served in World War II. Studied business interruption insurance while prisoner of war. Rejoined as policy drafter 1945 but resigned to join Inland Revenue 1946. Rejoined 1948. Life director, 1972; main board director 1981. Retired, 1983. p. 48, 58, 121, 126

Trigg, Bruce† – Joined Jauch & Hübener in Mülheim in 1976; transferred to international department, Frankfurt. Global property specialist, 1979; manager international department, Mülheim, 1985; PWG/UOC, 1992; board member, Jauch & Hübener retail, 1993; Aon, London, since 1998. p. 176, 182

Verbon, Herman – Joined Mees & zoonen in 1950. Succeeded Wim van der Have on PWG 1977. Left PWG in 1980. Retired 1986 p. 109

Westhorp, Ronald K. (Ronnie) – Joined Willis Faber in London from Griffiths Tait in 1960. From 1970 director responsible for incoming retail business from J&H. Founding member of PWG. Retired 1984. Died 2003. p. 106

Withers, Kenneth C. (Ken) – Joined J&H Brazil *circa* 1960; transferred to J&H Caracas. Country manager Venezuela, 1962. Country manager, Italy, 1966. J&H representative Willis Faber in London, 1968; J&H representative Brockman y Schuh, Mexico, 1974. Resigned 1976. Died early 1990s. p. 81, 82, 84

Zunino, Gianni* – Joined Willis Faber, London 1965. Left Willis Faber 1971 to join J&H Milan as casualty manager. J&H Hartford international manager, 1981. Managing director, 1997. Retired 2000. p. 84

Appendix II
References and further Reading

'Firm Foundations, The Origin of Willis Faber 1828–1928', Digby Brindle-Wood-Williams, unpublished

Gras Savoye, Une autre histoire du siècle, Ariane Fournier, Fragments editions, 2002

Jauch & Hübener 75 Years, Arno Surminski, Jauch & Hübener-Group PR Team, 1996

Johnson & Higgins at 150 Years, Richard Blodgett, Greenwich Publishing Group Inc., 1995

'Johnson & Higgins International Operations 1952–1972', Dorrance Sexton, unpublished

Private Line, 1979–1986, *Happenings*, 1986–1996: house magazines of Johnson & Higgins

Recollections of My Business Life, Edwin John Spencer, Hatchards, 1925

Review: house magazine of Willis Faber, Willis Faber Printing Services, 1970–1995

The Business and Battlecry, John Prentice, Alan Sutton Publishing, 1991

The Europeans, Luigi Barzini, Simon & Schuster, 1983